Inside the Lava Lamp

Inside the Lava Lamp

The Daughter's Tale

FRAN BAILEY

When her aging father asks for an enormous favour,
she agrees to do it. It takes her a long time,
but she finally does it . . . her way.

Copyright Fran Bailey

ISBN 978-1-0689273-0-0 (Print)
ISBN 978-1-0689273-1-7 (E-book)

Vankleek Hill, Ontario.

Printed by lulu.com

September 2024

Table of Contents

Jack	1
Jack's Manuscript	5
A Bit of Deception	7
Bella	13
The Farm	17
Wallpaper	25
The Farmette	27
The Bad Chapter	32
The Lodge	39
Compromises	43
Headphones and Head-bones	47
In the Beginning	49
Phyllis	59
Jack's War	63
A Couple of Glitches	69
Tombstone	71
Helga	74
The Villain	76
Party On	81
New Gadgets	83
His Last Train Ride	85
Northern Bliss	88
Raisins and the Male Cook	91
Francy and the Glasses	94
Magic	96
Lies and a Lesson for Life	99
Noodling	102
A Discovery	106
Walter	108
My Father's Bastards	110
Almost New Year's Eve	111
Celebration of Life	113
Dear Dad	115

*Though wise men at their end know dark is right
Because their words had forked no lightning, they
Do not go gentle into that good night.*

... Dylan Thomas

Chapter 1
Jack

Jack is a man whose words have forked a fair bit of lightning over his long life. Now, suddenly, he is motivated to hurl one more mighty thunderbolt while he still can. It has been a long time since he wrote that last novel, the one that *almost* got published.

Land of Triangles. I liked that title. He changed it though. Too bad. He wrote it when he was in his late sixties and it has been relegated to the top of his closet ever since that stinging let-down following a year of hope and encouragement from his agent. But now, galvanised anew by a remark from Nurse Lizzie, he wants to get the thing published. Correction. He wants *me* to get it published.

When Jack wrote his novel there was little access to self-publishing or vanity press, as he called it. Besides, he wouldn't have gone that route. No. He wanted to work with a real agent and get published by a real publishing house. So now I am to become his agent. It is a futile gesture but I agree to try.

Jack is very old now but in his mind he is young. Even though he has, in my opinion (and his as well), achieved a lot, there is always some new idea to try out. At ninety-five he still tries to plot and plan... and sometimes to meddle. Despite his diminished faculties: eyesight shot, hearing gone, mobility limited by arthritis, he persists in his efforts to realise his dreams. No, he is not going gentle.

For the past ten years Jack has been living at The Lodge, a seniors' home in the little Eastern Ontario town of Vankleek Hill. He relies on me for his extra needs and desires, which I can willingly fulfill because I live nearby. I am his daughter.

I visit my father often, always bearing treats like butter tarts or curd cheese or chocolate-covered cherries. He used to like creamed corn, cold, straight out of the tin, but recently I've noticed the same two tins rolling around in his sock drawer. It's possible his can opener has gone astray. It's amazing how things can go missing in such a tiny room.

Dad swears his diabetes has been cured, not believing that it's the meds that keep him from falling into a coma. Then there's the old prostate problem and he'll tell you all about that at every opportunity. "Oh hell, I've had prostate cancer for over forty years and look, I'm still here!" (Yes, because an orchiectomy was performed twelve years ago.) He also takes Effexor for depression or anxiety or general sadness that comes from living beyond one's body. As Willie Nelson reportedly said, "I've outlived my pecker!" Nailed it.

Jack was never a depressive type of person, he always bounced back from life's disappointments. But I know that his present physical restrictions are taking their toll. He takes one hell of a lot of medication. (Though sometimes I find the odd pill on his floor and toss it out with no apparent consequence.)

We gave him a special phone with huge blue numbers that light up but he still has trouble making calls. When he does succeed to reach me it's usually to ask for some simple thing like a six-pack of Coke (for the dry mouth) or a box of Carter's Little Pills (for the constipation) or a tube of rubber cement (to repair some broken thing). Mostly he wants my company. Just because he cannot see or hear well doesn't mean he cannot talk. He loves to talk, mainly about himself. I know all his stories and can fill in the blanks in his memory bank. He'll thump his head to indicate he's forgotten a name.

"When I was working at the canning factory in... (thump)

"Sainte Hyacinthe." I supply.

"...and I was going out with..." (thump)

"Claire"

"...that's it, and I was sharing an apartment with..."(thump)

"Doug"

"Right! Well, anyway, what was I saying?"

"Well, Dad, you asked me what's new and I was just about to tell you about..."

"Oh, so what's new?"

"George just had his eightieth birthday. He's now an octogenarian."

"What? He's auctioneering?!"

And so it goes.

Chapter 2
Jack's Manuscript

A few weeks ago, Dad called with an urgent request. I held the phone a foot away from my ear and could still hear his desperation. He huffed and puffed, "I want you to call those people at the blind place, you know...in Cornwall. I need one of those machines so I can read! You know what I mean! Like what Mom had. I've got to get my book published, god-dammit! There's a bad chapter I need to find and make some changes. It's in the wrong place. If I can find it and move it along toward the end, we can just make the Christmas market!"

I noticed the 'we'. It was mid-September and suddenly I am to become a literary advisor, perhaps agent, for an old man who is now legally blind. Sometimes when he really wants to read something he'll put on two pairs of glasses, one over the other, and also use his magnifying glass. This way he can make out a few words. And, knowing how determined he can be and seeing how charged up he is, I promise to call the CNIB and help him make his changes.

I soon learn the reason behind his sudden fervent desire to get his manuscript published. Nurse Lizzie. He likes to share his chocolate-covered-cherries with her. He has also shared his manuscript with her. She loves to read and if she reads as fast as she speaks, she must have read a lot of books.

Nurse Lizzie has asked him again when he's going to get his book published. "So you can sign my copy before...you know...before you croak."

Well, here we are now, mid-September and the Christmas book market looms. It's a race against time. Can I do it? Of course not. But I can *seem* to do it. And now it occurs to me that there is something else I can do.

Chapter 3
A Bit of Deception

I'm on the train, the VIA, heading west from Cornwall to Belleville for a short visit with my sister and brother-in-law. I love the train. Ideas come to me as we clatter along. It's a gorgeous autumn day and I lean my head against the window. I allow the passing landscape to mesmerise me. I am a painter and have enjoyed some success at local art shows and galleries. Commissions sometimes come my way. I begin to look at Dad's manuscript as another commission. How will I paint it?

We pass a section of swampy land, still very green. Old trees lie randomly where they fell. Younger trees, saplings, weave themselves over and around the dead trees. This is my template. I will weave my father's story into mine as I document our progress. This could work...a tapestry!

Now I am excited and discuss my scheme with Lynne and Frank when they meet me at the Belleville station. They are creatives too: actors, singers, writers, champions of new ideas. Their enthusiasm for what has become My Project encourages me. I realise I've been writing all my life. I have dozens of notebooks full of ideas, story beginnings, poems, plays. But because I cast myself in the role of painter I just never tried to get out of that box. We relax on their back deck in the late afternoon sun, sipping wine, watching the little stream sparkle below. "Bloody hell!" says Frank. "What a fantastic idea for a story! A story within a story."

"Yeah, " I say, "just like in Shakespeare! Can I have more wine?"

A week later I'm back at The Lodge. I meet Nurse Lizzie and explain to her just how very hard it is to get a book published. She understands and says, "The most important thing is to keep his spirits up. I've noticed that lately he hasn't been slamming his trays around so much in the dining room now that he has this project to keep him busy. He can get pretty cranky at times, especially if someone is in his way. I say to him, 'Jack, you can't just ram your wheelchair into people. You have to be more patient.' But he's calmed down a bit now, He seems happier. Let's hope it continues." Indeed!

Dad's room at The Lodge was next to the activities room. Whenever he wanted to wheel himself down to the main lounge he would be obliged to run a gauntlet through dart games or prayer services or yoga sessions. He was not shy about expressing his frustration while negotiating these roadblocks. Hannah, our intrepid yoga teacher, was surprised to learn that the cranky old guy in the wheelchair was my father.

Excerpt from Land of Triangles:

Well, Tyler died in the Northern Lights Inn, out on the Rolling Hills Strip, so one must put up with a certain amount of that. It is not unknown for older men to die in motel rooms. But he was more than just an older man. He was ninety-three, for god's sake! Shouldn't that make a difference? Have I been wrong to imagine that such longevity frees one at last of all primal appetite?

When he wrote that passage, I doubt he thought he'd make it to ninety-three, much less ninety-five. My father was never a health nut. He ate and drank pretty much as he liked, despite my mother's attempts to keep him to a sensible diabetic diet. To Dad, exercise was something other people did. He napped. He had this theory, among many, that the human body is like an automobile, its longevity governed by its mileage.

But by now he must have the answer to that last question. His own primal appetite still exists, if only in his mind. Longevity does not guarantee freedom of any kind.

His original title, Land of Triangles, comes from a poem by Tom MacInnes.

Last night in a land of triangles
I lay in a cubicle, where
a girl in pajamas and bangles
Slept with her hands in my hair.

There are more verses in this poem but I like the imagery of those first four lines which Jack used to introduce his story. The poem is called *Zalinka*. I found it the other day in one of his files marked "Poetry".

Jack used to keep immaculate files and records. Many of them now reside in our basement, along with so much of his other writing. His entries are informative and entertaining. Also in his poetry file is the story of The Blue Pumpkin, written on August 17, 1950. It's a very long epic-style poem designed to be read by him to Lynne and me in order to keep us safe inside the house on Halloween night.

Absent from the poetry file but etched indelibly in our minds is this little ditty he made up one evening while Lynne and I were waiting for Mom to finish shopping for groceries at the A&P. She always took a long time, chatting away with everyone, either in French or in English, depending on whom she met.

It was getting dark and we were getting hungry. Dad began to sing, to the tune of Rock of Ages:

Night is falling
Boom, bang, crash!
And tonight, we're having hash-
Dried up crusts and broken bones
and some soup that's made of stones...

By the time Mom finally appeared with the groceries we were all belting out the song from inside the car. I don't recall her reaction but we were singing ourselves silly.

Another file is marked 'Scrapbook' and it is just that, a random mix of unrelated but interesting facts.

<u>Such as</u>: information about one of Dad's favourite artists, Graham Norwell, (1901-1967) who was known for his paintings of the Laurentian Moun-

tains. Dad met Norwell some years after having seen and admired his paintings in a Montreal gallery window. He purchased two watercolours and has recently gifted them to Lynne and me. Lynne chose the one with cold dark waters surrounding snow-covered islands; I chose the one with the cabins nestled beneath a series of ski hills, possibly near St. Sauveur.

<u>Such as:</u> a list of old Fred Astaire musicals, including one of his favourites, Roberta.

<u>Such as</u>: a list of French proverbs translated into English. Here's one I like: *Revenons a nos moutons.* Let's get back to the subject.

Dad would have loved Google and Wikipedia but his internet days were limited to emails before macular degeneration frustrated even that much use of his computer. That and arthritic joints have combined to foil his management skills. I have rescued several file folders from the shambles of his present existence at The Lodge where papers tend to get shoved into odd spaces along with the remains of butter tarts. He does have a small filing cabinet but all it contains at the moment are boxes of tissues and a couple of harmonicas.

As I flip through another file marked 'Publishers' I discover all the ever-so-gentle rejection letters he received from the seventeen publishing houses his manuscript had visited. There must be a publishers' manual dealing with the hundreds of ways to say, "Thanks, but no thanks." As a balm to his own rejection, he includes within this folder a clipping from The Ottawa Citizen, August 29, 1993, written by Phil Jenkins who tells about the many well-known authors whose submissions were rejected sometimes more than twenty times before being accepted for publication. Among these were James Joyce, Robert Graves and E.E Cummings.

Chapter 4
Bella

That is the name of the literary agent Jack engaged. I know from the correspondence between them that she worked hard to find a publisher for his story. I wonder how she would feel if she knew that he chose her because of her name.

"What did I know about agents? Nothing! I simply browsed through The Canadian Writers' Market and when I saw the name Bella, I thought maybe she would bring me luck. You know who I am talking about, don't you?"

Yes, it was Bella M. She was such an important person in my father's young life, his first love. We never forget our first love, do we? Often, we are branded by it. In *Land of Triangles* Katherine is Bella.

"Do be still!" Katherine cried when he showed signs of too rapid arousal. "I'm just looking at your wound, for heavens' sake!" She pried up a corner of the bandage. "Yup! You're branded. When you grow new skin, it'll pucker. You can tell all your future girlfriends who branded you."

Last week while I visited him at The Lodge Dad pulled up his pant leg to show me the old scar just above his right knee. It was Bella M. who caused it. She had fired off a rifle, like you do when you are trying to impress someone. The bullet had ricocheted off a rail and grazed his thigh. I wonder how many future girlfriends got to see it.

Opening lines from *Land of Triangles:*

Katherine Willison has always had a vigorous character. She demonstrated this long ago by killing her father. She was fifteen at the time.

The detailed account of this event appears in Chapter Five. It's a pivotal scene, the one Dad now calls The Bad Chapter because MacMillan Publishing objected to *"...the mystery of the beach scene being revealed too soon."* But that scene was not the mystery of the story. The true mystery came near the end, where it belonged. Perhaps the reader at MacMillan was not compelled to read through to the end. A comment from McClelland & Stewart seems to confirm this. *"The main problem I had was that I couldn't engage with the characters sufficiently and felt only distantly involved with what happens to them."* A fair assessment, I think. I also found many of his characters sounded like the same person: Jack, or his alter-ego, Jonathan. Other criticisms include: *"...but I found the author's penchant for flashback made the plot seem lumbering."* (Hodder & Stoughton). Or: *"While we liked aspects of the novel, on balance we just weren't sufficiently enthusiastic..."* (A random comment from Random House.) And not all was negativity. *"I really enjoyed reading it. He writes extremely well. I don't think I can squeeze it in as a mystery. It's much more of a literary saga, in the best sense of the term."* (Such a positive negative from Charles Scribner's Sons.)

I had read Jack's story back in the mid-eighties when it was still called *Land of Triangles*. I'm not sure what happened nor why and when I asked Dad, he couldn't remember but by the time Bella sent it out to all those publishers the book had a new title.

Trainwatchers. In a way that made sense because of Dad's love for trains, but I didn't much care for it. Too close to *Trainspotting*, which is another kind of tale entirely, although Dad's story did involve cocaine later on in the plot. Also, most of the characters had new names. Katherine was now Isobel, Jonathan had morphed into Jamieson and the ninety-three year old C. Tyler Willison became Cecil Watchorn. But the story remained basically the same. As did a third incarnation called *The Carousel Racers*. To make things even more confusing each new version had revised dates. Originally Jonathan was born in the thirties but by the third version his character was a child of the sixties. This played hell with such references as "the new satellite, Sputnik" and the advent of diesel engines. But never mind. None of these manuscripts ever left Dad's desk. Just *Trainwatchers*.

Dad was fired up by his agent's initial enthusiasm. His hopes soared. He was sure his manuscript would be picked up. He had even asked me to illustrate the cover. I agreed although I knew that publishers have their own stable of artists for that purpose.

For months Dad floated on a cloud of anticipation. Would it sell? It HAD to! Maybe it would become a best-seller! He always dreamed big. He had already spent the money in his mind. A new car, a Crown Vic at least. Maybe a cruise. Oh, how he would flash it around!

We had all seen this pattern before. The elation followed by the let-down. Like the boat he almost bought. *A Richardson cruiser with room to sleep four in comfort and... a flying bridge!* Oh, the trips we would make down the St, Lawrence, up the Ottawa! I was ten and remember bragging to my friends about the boat we were going to get "with a flying bridge", whatever that was. The deal fell through. The guy who owned it had received a better offer and instantly became known as "that bastard McCorkindale". I soon learned not to count on good news until it really happened although sometimes, I found the anticipation more exciting than the result.

Disappointment reigned in our house for a few days but soon gave way to more practical matters. Dad decided to buy us a house instead. That summer we moved from our rented house in Ste. Annes to our mortgaged one in neighbouring Baie d'Urfe. We were all thrilled and the dream of big boats faded.

Now: Revenons a nos moutons.

When it became obvious that *Trainwatchers* was not going to fly, Dad's mood plummeted. But soon more immediate urgencies presented themselves. One thing about my father: he loves a good crisis.

Chapter 5
The Farm

Excerpt from my father's log book dated May 1969, just months before the moon landing:

How did it start? What has led us to auctions? Is it a form of rural osmosis?

It was early evening at the end of a road in East Hawkesbury Township, Prescott County. Horses in the field. A man told us his brother-in-law owned it, had inherited it from his great aunt. It was for sale.

July 1969: *A telephone call from Bill...he is now agreeing that perhaps his first asking price was a little high. Maybe he might think some about something in the $12,000 area. So, we go back for a better look.*

December 1969: *Bill and I have talked. It's practically a deal--$8500 with ten acres.*

April 1970: *Quebec election today. We voted at 9:15. Liberal landslide! Everybody cautiously ecstatic.*

May 1970: *Hudson house has sold.*

And so it happened. My parents crossed the Quebec border to live in Eastern Ontario. They were at the forefront of the mass exodus that was beginning due to rumblings of political unrest in Quebec. A few years later, when Rene Levesque and the Separatists won, hordes of Anglos fled up highway 401 to live and work in Toronto. This political situation was one factor in my father's decision to leave the province but the bigger motivation was his sense of adventure and fulfilment of his long-held dream to live in the country and restore an old house. This was a popular trend in the early seventies, regardless of politics. Sales of paint stripper and sandpaper soared.

The Farm was an old Gothic Revival farmhouse in need of much work.

Undeniably there is some charm there. Also, a lot of weeds, a rickety bridge over the stream, no sides to the bridge. Really now, doesn't it look a bit Tobacco Road-ish?

Their friends, George and Barb, had made a similar move a few years earlier, from the suburbs of Toronto to a country 'estate' near Lake Simcoe. They drove down one weekend to help assess and advise.

Barbara: "I like it, I like it!"

(But the beams in the cellar?)

Barbara: "It's nothing, it's nothing!"

(But the stucco?)

Barbara: "It's nothing, it's nothing!"

There was, of course, a lot of junk to be removed. Dad had hired a man to do the job. Dad was used to things being done on time. That's how he worked and that's how he expected others to work. He would find out that this city principle didn't apply in the country.

Aurele kept promising to show up with his truck, but 1) his truck needed repairs, 2) his 'man' went on a bender and didn't show up for three days. 3) his replacement couldn't come Thursday because he ran out of rabbit food and he had to stay home to slaughter all his rabbits.

Slowly, but slowly, my parents toiled away. This was their big project, a labour of love and, I think, one of the only things that kept them together. My sister and I had long since left home by then. We were living our own lives but we did enjoy visiting The Farm, especially in the early days when the house was a work-in-progress. A carnival atmosphere prevailed. Plaster dust and sawdust filled the air as each room underwent its own particular metamorphosis, emerging from years of neglect into quiet Victorian splendour.

The large dining room had a chair-rail around its perimeter and wallpaper was in the plans to cover the dingy blue walls. But before the papering was done, we all had a bit of fun. Magic markers were generously placed along the chair-rails, like chalk at a blackboard. Anyone who visited was encouraged to write or draw something directly on the walls. We were writing status updates years before Face Book. By the end of that first year the dining room walls were completely covered with graffiti. Whoever begins to strip that wallpaper in the future will be in for a bit of a giggle.

An impressive fieldstone fireplace emerged from behind the bricks in the country kitchen. Across its mantel, Dad arranged his prized set of six antique bulls-eye glass oil lamps. Upstairs the original claw-footed bathtub now sat upon a dais under which ran the new bathroom plumbing. The ceiling over the bathtub sloped, making it necessary to crouch while exiting the tub, especially for a tall person. The walls of this bathroom received a covering of red and black flocked wallpaper, reminiscent of a glorious bordello. Downstairs a powder room was installed between the living and dining rooms with a door on each side. Within the powder room was a space under the front stairs which became a small cupboard. My young sons kept their toys there and called it Henny Penny's Cave. At the top of the main staircase was a large hallway, beautifully lit by a Gothic window. My mother immediately claimed this space as her sewing nook and began running up curtains and stripey farmer-girl overalls for herself to wear.

Excerpt from the logbook, September 12, 1970:

Worked on Gothic window. Outside. Worked a great deal on my courage and got it to a point where I dared to make extension legs for the stepladder. After lashing it with ropes to the window I got on top and damned-well painted the topmost peak, gingerbread and all. I am very proud of myself.

October 4, 1970:

Worked on winterising the back porch. Every goddamned time I climbed up on the roof it started to rain. I nailed, sawed, calked, hammered, broke my sabre saw, cursed, swore, pounded fingers, jammed hand on caulking gun and finally quit at 4 pm when Doris and Guy arrived. We polished off his heel of rye. Then we polished off my heel of rye. Then we ate squash soup and baked squash.

Dad also roto-tilled a large garden plot for Mom to plant her vegetables. As in everything she did, she took gardening very seriously. Of course, she overdid the squash that first year. I remember coming home from work one afternoon to discover an arsenal of zucchinis, each the size of a small torpedo.

Their first winter at The Farm was a doozie, as anyone who experienced the record-breaking snowfall of March, 1971 will confirm. Dad, in his early fifties, was still commuting to work in Ste. Annes. He had to contend with a very long, very narrow driveway, originally intended for horse and buggy. There were many ditchings that winter of both car and tractor. Other bad things happened.

December 10, 1970:

It has been One of Those Days. As I was coming home, I slid slowly off the edge of my badly-plowed driveway and into my snow-filled ditch. I got the tractor, inserted front-end-loader under rear end of car, lifting it up quite handily and at the same time puncturing my gasoline tank in two places. I let her settle down again and watched 18 gallons of gasoline drain onto the snow.

More ditchings would follow, some involving other peoples' vehicles.

January 2, 1971:

For Christ's Sake! Today utter strangers got ditched in our driveway! Ha Ha Ha! Yesterday we even had a horse in our ditch. What bloody-well next?
   There were some good moments, though.

January 10, 1971:

Such wonderful insanity! Tonight...a still, cold evening...full moon...huge soft snow flakes. I plowed the driveway, then wandered off into the deep snow near the train tracks. Made an angel in the snow. I studied the moon and watched an owl swoop down looking for mice. Listened to the crackling silence of winter. Heard the far, far wail of the Canadian, felt it getting closer, saw its headlights bathe the snow until it thundered by about twenty feet from where I lay. After the noise and light faded, I arose and floundered back to the house.

March 3, 1971:

Here we lie, awaiting the onslaught of yet another storm. Will we be able to get out tomorrow? Depends, I suppose, on the driveway. That ever-present-ominous-all-life-contracting-son-of-a-bitch-of-a-snow-channelled, drift-catching-vehicle-ditching-bastard-of-a-driveway.

March 4 1971:

This day has made history of a sort. Upon

awakening, I looked out the window and said "the hell with it" and went back to bed. No roads are open. Montreal is paralysed; no trains, no planes... nothing! Here the drifts are beyond description... our north dining room window is drifted up to the topmost pane.

I remember that day very well. I was stranded at home in Hudson with my year-old son. His father was stranded in Montreal. Pierre Trudeau had just married Margaret Sinclair and were happily enjoying each other in the Rockies. It was my twenty-seventh birthday.

Like good pioneers my parents made it through that first winter. A few years later, after the major work was done, they opened an antique shop in the loft over the shed. On weekends they haunted auction sales in search of treasures they could restore and resell. A sign, **Victoria House Antiques**, now hung at the end of the long, now-improved driveway. Victoriana was their specialty, especially Eastlake furniture. They also adopted a black lab and called him Victor.

Family, friends and customers visited. The shelves and display cases up in the loft filled with treasures rescued from estates whose owners had no more use for them. It was a recycling bonanza, a bounty of crockery wash-stand sets, pressed-glass tableware in pinks and greens, silver-plate cutlery, hydro insulators (unthreaded being highly prized), and clocks. Lots of wooden clocks that Dad would wind regularly, all ticking and bonging, never quite in unison.

We began to refer to the house and my parents as The Farm, as in, "Let's go to The Farm." Or, if they came to visit us, "Here comes The Farm." My sons have wonderful memories of The Farm, especially the creek which meandered through the property where they could feed the fish from the little bridge or skate in winter. The Farm was an exciting and satisfying chapter in our family's life.

But, as we know, nothing lasts forever, neither the good nor the bad. After twenty-two years it was time to sell The Farm. The long driveway seemed longer, especially in winter. The general upkeep of the house became more challenging for a man now in his mid-seventies. Nearly falling off the roof convinced him of that.

The plan had always been to stay there until my grandmother died. Mamoe had slowly come to love it there despite strong early misgivings. "Your father is crazy! He's too old for that nonsense...have you seen the house? It's a mess! Who needs it?" Of course, Mamoe moved to The Farm with my parents and enjoyed its every aspect, from her lavender bedroom to Victor the dog, who became the happy recipient of Mamoe's sneaky treats, to 'helping' customers in the shop. She became famous for her comment, "Who needs it?"

Mamoe died in April 1992 at age ninety. The Farm was sold in June.

It was at The Farm that my father wrote *Land of Triangles*.

Chapter 6
Wallpaper

It's interesting how the mind works, how sometimes one thought leads to another not-exactly-related thought. We're now near the end of March, six months since the start of this writing project. Dad has accepted that we have missed the deadline for the Christmas market. He appreciates my efforts to get his book out. I still haven't told him the truth about what I am doing. Today we are just having a chat about other things. I ask him where his harmonica is.

"Oh, it's in the desk drawer...or maybe the filing cabinet. Sometimes when those terrible fiddlers come by, they ask me to play with them. The trouble is that when George fixed it he put it together backward. It's a bit difficult to play that way."

"Oh dear...I know George does have that tendency. He often does things backward or upside down. He becomes so intent on the project that he often misses the big picture. I remember once he wallpapered the bathroom...so pleased to show me when I got home. He didn't notice that the flowers were hanging down from their stems. At least the seams matched."

"Your mother, though, she was a master at hanging wallpaper. Meticulous at matching and going around corners. She'd spend hours up a ladder, making the joins so perfect, even if nobody else could see them. I loved those early days when we were both working on the restorations. And that main staircase! Wasn't it magnificent? The easy rake of it, the gleaming woodwork of the balustrades. And what I really enjoyed was that I could take a pee off the front porch and nobody could see...or care! God, I loved that place!

Chapter 7
The Farmette

They moved to a smaller side-split in the same area. It was a nice house but it wasn't The Farm. A year after this downsize adjustment, they learned that the house had a faulty foundation. It would have to be removed from its moorings, set down for a spell in the back yard while the new fly-ash-free foundation was poured, then repositioned. This procedure took over three months to complete. I heard Dad mutter the word 'parging' quite a lot during that operation. Mom and Dad found lodgings with a widower in town with whom they both got along. The other good news was that Dad's insurance covered all the costs.

The bad news? Well, I think this unsettling episode on top of her mother's death (though not untimely), followed by the sudden move to a smaller house (a necessary wrench), on top of the fact that George and I had decided to move to Vancouver Island...these major changes might have contributed to Mom's increasingly strange behaviour.

Dementia comes on slowly. At first, we just laughed it off when Mom said or did odd things. I remember one Thanksgiving when Lynne and I were visiting. We suddenly realised there would be no dinner unless we both got busy. Yes, there was a turkey but it was still out in the garage, waiting. Mom seemed quite content to let us take over her kitchen. It was as if she was the visitor, not us. Not that we minded helping out, it's just that Mom had always had things under control. This time she just sat back and relaxed, enjoying our company and appreciating our efforts. As usual, Lynne and I were making silly sisterly remarks, having a few laughs, at anything and nothing. Mom said, "I know I say silly things sometimes. I don't mind if you laugh, it's okay." We weren't laughing at her...well, maybe a bit, but she was kind enough to approve. I think she was aware of the changes.

On October ninth, 1999, we celebrated their sixtieth wedding anniversary at The Farmette. Mom had kept a yearly diary since 1983 but failing eyesight and early confusion meant her 1999 diary was her last. Here is her entry for October ninth:

Celebration! Our daughters want us out while they take over the kitchen. Jack took me to Harden's to look at the polar bear etched in the diamond he gave me. It was hard to see. Then to Lise for a haircut, then to Mariette for a fuchsia blouse. Had a sandwich at Mary's. Home all decorated. Food cooking. Everyone here! Good music and family-oriented gifts as sixty years are celebrated. Bless the hands that made it possible!

At The Farm there was no dishwasher but The Farmette had one. Mom refused to use it. Too complicated. Dad had bought her a cordless phone to use while she was out in the garden but she wouldn't use that either. At first, we thought she was just being stubborn. It was more than that.

In 2000 George and I returned from our six-year adventure on Vancouver Island. We found a house near The Farmette, halfway between Hawkesbury and Vankleek Hill. We were just in time to notice that Mom's strange behaviour was getting worse. She had stopped driving, blamed it on her poor eyesight. Who could argue with that? She enjoyed it when I took her shopping for groceries but I noticed how she would watch what I put into my basket, then put the same items into hers. One day as I dropped by to pick her up, I heard this heated argument coming from the living room. Mom was shouting at Dad, "You can't make me take those fucking pills!" I was stunned. I got her into the car and listened to her rant about Dad, how he was a hermit, he didn't take her anywhere, he didn't go out. None of this was true. He was trying his best to keep her happy. I knew it was time to act.

It wasn't Alzheimer's. Brain scans indicated small strokes. Vascular dementia. She was eighty-one. And so began trips to the memory clinic and general misery. It meant another move would be necessary in the near future. Mom was unable to care for herself or for the house. Once so house-proud I would now find her in the kitchen, going through drawers, sweeping the floor or doing laundry without using soap. There were strange and dangerous food concoctions in the fridge that I would turf, lettuce in the freezer, meat in the crisper, rotting. I noticed how small she was becoming.

There was a heartbreaking moment when Lynne and her family came down to join in Dad's birthday celebration. My son, Jon, arrived from Montreal with a DVD copy of one of Dad's favourite musicals,

Roberta. Dad had explained how Lynne's first name was Roberta because of the movie. Everyone was at the dining room table and as I entered from the kitchen with the cake, I heard Mom say to Lynne, "Isn't that funny...I have a daughter named Roberta Lynne too!" I lit the candles; we sang Happy Birthday to Dad and I saw the tears in my sister's eyes.

It was a painful and frustrating time. Many bottles of wine were consumed as Dad and I thrashed out various plans of action. Sometimes George would take Mom out for a drive, which she loved. It gave me a chance to liberate her fridge from fungus and her cupboards from small weevils and flying things. Stephanie's Restaurant became the only solution for daily meals. They had their own booth and favourite waitress, Louise. Dad loved this part, of course. Often, he would ask George and me to join them; our company guaranteed a reason to order a martini and a bottle of wine.

We hired a cleaning woman. Sylvie would wash the kitchen floor and then take a smoke break outside on the patio. I don't think any more cleaning was done after that but it didn't matter because Mom enjoyed chatting with Sylvie. She knew nothing about Mom; therefore, she couldn't challenge anything Mom said.

Dad had by now taken over the daily diary entries. His last entry for 2000:

Our guests didn't show up for our New Years' Revels and we don't know why. Oh well, Happy New Year!

No guests had been invited.

Things continued like this for the next year but the spectre of a seniors' residence was on the horizon. One night Dad awoke to find Mom in his bedroom, sitting on his desk. She thought she was in the bathroom. Soon after that The Farmette went up for sale.

Chapter 8
The Bad Chapter

"It's quite simple.", he said, "We just have to find that bad chapter that comes too soon and shunt it closer to the end."

This was Dad's simple solution to make his manuscript saleable. Just shunt the bugger. How hard could it be?

Well, here it is, Chapter 5 of Land of Triangles a.k.a Trainwatchers.

1959, June 24

Here is the picture seen by Luke Pooney...

We have Jonathan and Kate, naked on Redwater Beach, her father some hundred yards distant. They run to the boat. but at the last moment she spins away, sprints back and tackles her father just as he aims. A thundering shot splashes the water behind the skiff, drifting out now, carrying Jonathan, alone and naked. His clothes are in a sad little pile behind Bradley Willison, who has dropped the rifle now and grabbed Kate with his left hand. His right begins a tattoo of slaps across her face.

She strikes out, once, twice, and her father staggers drunkenly, but recovers fast, pinions her, squeezing. He pays no heed to the boy in the boat offshore. He forces Kate into the sand until he has her pinned on her back, helpless. All at once he is kneeling between her legs in a most unfatherly manner. She breaks free and claws his face. He slaps her viciously and presses a forearm across her chest, bearing down to cut off her breathing. He forces himself into the widening spread of her legs, settling himself solidly between them.

Luke Pooney is filled with a mad fascination. He is barely aware of Jonathan's difficulty getting back to shore. He is on the edge of panic, unable to believe what he is seeing. This obscene humping form is an illusion. It is impossible that he is seeing her father. He cannot take his eyes off the scene, yet he can't completely ignore the boat, now scraping sand as Jonathan leaps ashore with that little .22 rifle. He runs up the beach.

All at once Luke is aware that Jonathan's arrival has distracted Bradley Willison momentarily, for he looks up, off-guard for just a second-a vital second, for in that second Katherine explodes. The suddenness of her action throws her father off while she rolls to one side, slamming into the 30-30 lying in the sand. Then she erupts, face tear-stained and bloody. Now she holds the rifle.

Luke watches her father rise too, staggering again, and even from that distance he sees horror on Willison's face. He looks wildly from Kate to Jonathan who has moved protectively in front of Kate. Luke savours a grotesque bewitchment as Kate sweeps Jonathan aside with the barrel of the 30-30. She moves the barrel up and aims at a point somewhere above her father's knees. Luke hears him scream, "Kate! For Christ's sake..."

The world explodes with a deafening blast. He is struck to the ground. He is still for a few seconds. Then his hands move, feebly grabbing at his own genitals.

Kate moves closer, breathing in great, racking sobs. Her moans of detestation are audible, even at that distance. She handles that rifle with purpose. She snaps the lever action and a spent shell twinkles in the sunlight. The lever closes with a metallic clang. She moves the muzzle up and holds it directly at his head. He screams, tries to crawl away. The muzzle follows his every move. She screams too. Her message is simple: "I told you <u>never</u> to try that!"

She squeezes the trigger. Luke hears the click of the firing pin on an empty chamber. Kate yells, "Shit!", with no little heat. If Bradley hadn't blasted off that third shot at the skiff he'd be dead as that whiskey-jack that Kate had shot earlier.

Now she has the rifle by the barrel, bringing it up to smash her father's head. Jonathan wrests it from her. She screams at him, her hands become claws-- but instead of attacking she crumples to the sand in a dead faint. It was enough to make Luke reach his uncontrollable climax. Then he watched Jonathan cover his nakedness with his swimming trunks after throwing both rifles far up on the beach. It never occurred to Luke that he might go down and help. It wasn't his problem.

Jonathan looked at the groaning form of Kate's father, then at the crumpled Kate, who seemed to be out cold. He carries her to the blanket by the small fire, places her on one side and covers her up with the other. He moistens a handkerchief and wets her forehead. Luke, still watching, thinks, "Just like in the movies." He saw Kate stir slightly and wondered what it would feel like to slide his fingers between her legs.

He watched Jonathan go to work on Kate's father. He eventually succeeds in wrestling him into the bow of the skiff. Luke watches in stunned surprise as the little skiff takes off and heads for the railway trestle. Kate is left behind! Oh, now!

Luke is overwhelmed by a hard-driving prurient anticipation. His erection is back and there is Kate, not three hundred feet away, practically naked and ready for action…sure, she is! And Luke is just the boy to see that she gets it.

And now…what about Jonathan?

He doesn't really like Bradley Willison, but you can't just sit around and watch a man bleed to death. Which might happen anyway, no matter what is done if the deepening crimson of the bilge-water is any indication.

The only hope is an aircraft that might get him to Eastport in time. There is usually at least one plane up at the fire ranger's headquarters farther along the north arm of Redwater Lake. So Jonathan returns to the railway trestle. To save time he takes the dangerous short-cut across the small bay. Jonathan runs wide open, ignores a new vibration in the control handle and transom of the boat. He doesn't know Bradley's second shot had struck his propeller.

There is a plane at the forestry station. They take Bradley from the boat. He explains, between groans, that it has been an accident. His eye catches the boy, *pleading silence as he gasps, "I tripped...I fell...on my rifle." He passes out cold. They look at Jonathan who nods dumbly. And so, the lie is established.*

They load him into the aircraft and Jonathan slips away from the confusion. He doesn't want to talk about the matter, not right now. He is half a mile down the lake when the plane takes off. It rises from the water ahead of him, banks to the south and sets off for Eastport.

Now Jonathan can concentrate on immediate matters. His first concern is for the motor. Although he wants to get back to Kate quickly, he knows he must not risk the short-cut beyond the trestle. He must keep the motor well-below half speed. Still, there is a worrisome shake. It makes the bilgewater dance with curiously inverted droplets glistening in the sun. They are quite red.

The sun was much lower when he got back to the beach. Kate had wakened, had put more wood and cedar boughs on the fire. And a good thing too. Black flies get more vicious as evening approaches and mosquitoes come out. She sat huddled on the blanket, staring at absolutely nothing. She was not in good shape. Blood from the fly bites mixed with blood from the attack. Her left eye was puffed and she was badly bruised in several places.

She was still naked. She did not want to speak.

Jonathan washed her as tenderly as he could, feeling like an imbecile because he had not been able to prevent this double outrage. He cried softly to himself as he helped her to dress. He couldn't understand her when she first spoke because her voice came out as a rasping whisper. "Why did you help him, Jonathan? I want him dead! Can't you get that into your stupid goddamned head?"

He was overpowered by her sad and hopeless desperation; by the killing look in her eyes. He shivered and pulled away. There was little else he could do for her and he had to clean the skiff. He drew it up on the shore, removed the motor and saw the damaged propeller blade. He sluiced down the sides and the forward seat with the bailing bucket. he got most of the blood off, canted the boat and let the bloodied water drain into the sand. He could do nothing about the propeller so he decided to chance it. Slowly. He helped Kate into the boat and they crawled back at the lowest possible speed.

The trip took forever. It was dark when they passed under the railway trestle into the North Arm. A faint hazy moon cast a ghostly aura over Windigo Island as they crept by. When they cleared a small point of land they were both startled by a pair of fire flares about a mile and a half ahead of them. Almost at the same instant a float plane came in for a landing, so low they both ducked.

Arriving at the dock the same time as Uncle Tyler in the Norseman was the greatest surprise of all. It was the first time Jonathan had seen him since the arrival last December. Under ordinary circumstances he would have been impressed by the vivid dynamism that was the trademark of the man, together with a radiating sense of warmth and power. But now he was only mildly surprised and, to Jonathan, the big consideration was---how in hell did he get there so fast?

Well, all things considered, it had been a hell of a way to spend a sixteenth birthday.

Chapter 9
The Lodge

It all happened fast, as it always did with major events involving my father. The real estate agent sold the house before the sign went up. The auctioneer assessed the contents of the house. She especially admired the Tiffany lamp and the Lalique vases so they had to be part of the swag. Dad thought they might fetch a small fortune. They did not.

I attended the auction with Dad. It was brutal seeing some of those memories get snatched up by the bargain hunters but turnabout is fair play: my parents were once the bargain hunters during their antique shop days. The oak dining room set had two parties bidding on it so it gave a good return, as did the bombe glass-fronted china cabinet. The rest was underwhelming.

George took Mom out for a drive while we were at the auction and the movers carted off the remaining furniture to The Lodge. We all met there and set about placing the few familiar pieces in their new "home". Mom took it quite well. Dad was more interested in the final tally from the auction.

One of the items I got to keep was the coverlet Mom had worked on over the long years of their marriage but had never got around to completing herself. It was called a yo-yo quilt; made up of hundreds of cotton circles, gathered around the edges to form a little puff. These puffs were then sewn together. The fabrics used had once been dresses, blouses, aprons and such. The colours were multi, the patterns charming. Mom never got around to stitching all the sections together so they had travelled, in the bottom drawer of her dresser, to all the various homes my parents had lived in.

An unfortunate happening took place while the quilt, still in sections, was at The Farm. Mamoe decided it would be a wonderful surprise to have the quilt finally put together. She knew some ladies who were quilters. One day when Mom was away Mamoe stealthily gathered the pieces and handed them over for the ladies to finish. It was to be a birthday surprise. The ladies did quite a number on that quilt. After piecing it together they attached it to a pea green backing and added an edging of little pea green pointy bits. Mamoe proudly presented this to Mom, in anticipation of joyful delight. Deadly silence. Phyllis was not pleased. She continued to silently dislike the offering while Dad tried to explain to Mamoe that, nice gesture and all, it was not her place to decide when or how or *if* the quilt should be finished. I think Mom had her reasons for not finishing the quilt; that was her business. She eventually got over her snit and placed the quilt on the spool bed in the guest bedroom.

I recently spent one winter picking apart the stitching and re-attached a darker background to the quilt, which made the colours pop. I also turfed the pointy edging. But the fabric is too old to sit on my bed with cats clawing at it so, again, it sits alone in a drawer once more.

My parents took up residence in a two-room suite at The Lodge. Mom had always liked being with people and singing so she felt comfortable in her new surroundings. She could get away with trivial chit-chat amongst the other residents. One of her favourite throw-away lines became, "Chacun a son tour a l'assiette au beurre." (Everyone has a turn at the butter dish." And who could argue with that? At times she would belt out this ditty:

It was great-
We were late-
Nobody cared how much we ate
At the Jewish Wedding
Jubilee-ee-ee!

The Lodge provided a lot of activities for the residents. Dad was good at darts and won the 'championship' a few times. Mom joined the exercise group. Sitting on chairs the residents would lift weights or swing their legs to music. One day I joined in on one of these sessions. At the end, during the cool-down, our leader, a new girl with a nose-ring and pink hair, made the following suggestion." Okay, now everybody, turn to the person to your left and tell them how much you love them." All heads obediently turned left and spoke lovingly to the back of their neighbour's head. The young girl realised her mistake and tried again. "Okay, now everybody, call out a number like this, 'one, two, one two, all around the circle. If you're a one you turn to the right, if you're a two you turn left. Let's try it again."

Fortunately, it was lunch time so everyone wandered off to the dining room, chanting, "one, two, one, two."

Dad was still able to function normally at the time of their arrival at The Lodge. He loved to read, write and drive. He took Mom on a trip to Thunder Bay that first year. On their way back they stopped in for a visit with Lynne and Frank in Toronto. During the night Mom got up for a pee, then climbed back into bed...with her son-in-law. It was a brief encounter and cause for a few giggles in the morning.

Back at The Lodge, Dad tried to get back to his writing. Mostly he was working on new titles for Land of Triangles a.k.a. Trainwatchers. Here is a sampling of some of his ideas: My Sweetie Went Away...The Cannibal King of Paradise...Devil on a Level Field...Leghorn Cock ...Soul of Mud...Not Wholly Dead...The Unexploded Man

He would ask my opinion of each new title. I would reply honestly: "Blecch!"

Chapter 10
Compromises

Here is a poem I found among Jack's writing files. I think he wrote it while he was working on his manuscript and reliving old memories of Bella M.

I've kept it quiet since many years ago-
That first sweet love, I've kept it always
like a tiny feeble glow,
smouldering within me, burning still.
A background to my soul, a muted song,
It woke again last night in muted dreams,
Burst into blazing searing heat
Of long remembered passion, torment and remorse,
Frustration too, mingled, blended, passing in review.
The bittersweet of unforgotten love,
Old thoughts of you.

It was during this time he tried to find her. He didn't have internet access back then but he did find her phone number. He called. Her husband answered. He told Jack that Bella had changed, that she wasn't the young girl he had known, that she didn't want to meet him. Jack, of course, was crushed and angry. He had last seen Bella in 1937 when he was twenty-one. She was studying to be a nurse in Kingston, he was traveling around on trains between Quebec and Ontario, seeking his fortune. He describes their last meeting in his memoir titled **Mutations of a Mind.**

Things were once again all right in our world: the slowly widening rift magically closed and we were together again. Inside-our-heads-together. As we had been for years. We talked a blue streak and of course I had brought my magazine with my story in it and Bella conceded that I might not become a bum. She advised me to go where my writing took me. We sat together on the sofa and the clock zoom-rushed to train time. There was still so much unsaid, so much undone. Stupidity was still my operating mode but Bella compensated for that. She held my face in her two hands and kissed me. Meltdown! That kiss became a yardstick for many years. But...nothing is forever.

Maybe that kiss and the hoped-for consequences, though unrealised, was part of the reason.

Maybe Mom had carried a torch as well, one that smouldered in that secret place she nurtured. I found a letter at the bottom of her box of keepsakes from a young man called Darroch who had promised to write again as soon as he was stationed in Britain. The letter was dated 1937, two years before my parents married.

Whatever the reason, by the time they were in their forties my parents were living as brother and sister.

"I loved your mother so much but we never really discussed intimate things. We just drifted into this limbo of avoiding sex. I don't know why."

"Well, Dad, I think she liked having other people living in the house, especially after Lynne and I left home. It protected her from having any real intimacy with you, either physical or emotional. When you think back there was always someone from her clan living with you: her sister, her brother, her mother, even her grandmother, Memere. She needed them as a buffer."

But they stayed together as part of an early unspoken pact. Having come from broken homes themselves it was paramount for them to create a stable environment for their little family. On the surface they succeeded but in my personal experience it was often a hollow model.

In **Trainwatchers** Kate says, *Life is often a second-best kind of thing. It's a compromise between the ideal and the possible. I've learned to put up with it, that's all."*

When they moved to The Farm, Dad was still working and had a long commute, so he rented an apartment in Montreal where he stayed during the week. This freed him to pursue other interests. He set up a small N-Gage model railway there. He also had a girlfriend. He was discreet about her. The convenience of his apartment made everyone happy, including Mom, who was content to grow her vegetables, attend meetings of the Women's' Institute, to volunteer at the hospital and to serve customers in the antique shop. She enjoyed her role as chatelaine of Victoria House.

Did she know about the girlfriend? Yes. Did it bother her? Not a bit.

Chapter 11
Headphones and Head-bones

On my next visit to The Lodge, I attempt to read some of Dad's manuscript to him. First, I have to change his hearing-aid batteries...those damned things don't last long enough. He has three hearing-aids of different makes and he refuses to wear the left one but it's futile to argue with him over such a silly quirk.

I begin reading, "Katherine was now in the medical publishing business...."

"What!? Did I write that? Oh Jeezus, my head-bone isn't working...I don't remember any of that. Who the hell is Katherine?"

Oh dear. This isn't going to work. And I'll be hoarse from shouting if I continue to read loud enough for Dad to hear me. So, I make a decision. I will read each chapter into a recorder. Dad can listen on headphones at his leisure, then we can discuss changes. He will be satisfied that we are doing something while at the same time I will begin to write my own manuscript, documenting the experience. This might work. He doesn't need to know about this part. Not yet.

It is now mid-October and I am dictating chapter two of *Land of Triangles*, a.k.a. *Trainwatchers*. Chapter one is with Dad to be used at his convenience. It will be a long slog to the final chapter. We're definitely not going to make the Christmas market.

It was December 9, 1958, the day of TIU, a northern god of war. That's quite fitting considering the eruptions that started as soon as our family got off the train at the bitter Northern Ontario station of Hector. I remember leaving Charles Street in Toronto and how I cried because the move frightened me.

Chapter 12
In the Beginning

Jack was born in 1916 above a butcher's shop in Toronto. The dates on his parents' marriage certificate suggests that he was a love-child. This notion appeals to his romantic nature. Jessie Gavin, his mother, a lass from Aberdeen Scotland, was alone during the birth. His father, Valentine Smith, born in Sheffield, England, was somewhere in France, in a trench. He died of pneumonia a year after Jack's birth, never having seen his son.

John Smith: that was my father's unremarkable name. Dad claims to be able to remember his earliest existence as being *something as simple and comforting as a lava-lamp; think of it...brilliant colours erupting in slow blobs like a psychedelic cloud, expanding and descending, to rise again with colour even more splendid. My earliest dreams were like that. I was inside, part of the action, not an observer. I was the motion, the colour, the warmth and soft comfort. These must have been dreams of the womb, of pre-birth. A fading memory of life before life. The wonder of it...the mystery...*

Wow! Just like Salvador Dali, my father remembers being inside the womb. Or maybe he had read Dali's words and appropriated them.

But the mystery of a lava lamp is only a piece of wax heated by a coil inside an odd objet d'art from the sixties. It has no real significance. Nor has the story of my life; biography is a bore and usually quite dishonest. It's too easy to leave out the warts.

Life is simply change and I'd rather talk about that. It'll be a lot more fun to take a slice of specific time and see how it is modified, edited, mutated into something else.

I'M TOLD IT WAS A GENTLER TIME IN 1916...

That was true if you ignored a World War and Germans attacking Verdun in February, hammering it 'til almost Christmas, by which time over a million and a half men had fallen and nothing won. I was about five months old when the last Verdun victim was done in.

He also remembers moving around a lot while he and his mother lived in Toronto. They lived in a succession of rooming houses on streets including Charles, Dartnell, Dovercourt and Gloucester.

In Toronto the streets were uncluttered by automobiles, some were muddy, others were paved, all of them dotted with thousands of pounds of horse manure every day. There was an aroma in the air too, heavier and darker than horse manure. It came from the pall of smoke hanging everywhere. Quite natural. All houses and factories used coal. Ten thousand tons of coal consumed in Toronto every day, most of it bituminous, the real black-smoke kind. That was Toronto...horse manure and smoke.

Yet automobiles were coming along too. I heard an 'uncle' say the gasoline engine car was a pollution-free answer to the problem of smoke and horse manure.

Jack also remembers going to revival meetings

with his mother and several of her Scottish friends.

We sang a catchy song:
Nothing to pay, no, nothing to pay,
Jesus will come and show us the way,
Free is the ticket; climb on today,
Toronto to glory...and nothing to pay!

Suspicion born when they passed the collection plate during this refrain.

I was included in these events because the term 'baby-sitter' hadn't been coined yet and neither had the idea. Rich people had nurses and maids; the poor dragged their kids everywhere...which was not that bad. It let me hear about all kinds of interesting events while I sprawled on the floor, drawing and listening.

I heard juicy stuff about Ruth Snyder and Judd Gray, right from their murder of Ruth Snyder's husband to their execution.

I heard about the latest suicide vogue of jumping off the Bloor Street Viaduct into the Don Valley.

I heard about 'returned soldiers' all the time, and shell-shock, which made them get drunk and beat their wives.

There was also a succession of 'uncles'. The one Jack remembers is Uncle Walter who gifted young Jack with an electric train. That was hard to beat. But then along came Albert Deragon, who gave young Jack a kaleidoscope...a wonderful mystery until he opened it up to see what was inside. Three trashy mirrors and a handful of coloured glass.

When Jack was ten his widowed mother married 'uncle' Albert Deragon. They moved around a lot more and ended up in the northern railway divisional point called Jellicoe. It wasn't even a village. It was a cold and primitive dot on the map, north of Lake Superior and far from anything resembling what they had been used to in the city. A box-car was their first home. When babies began to arrive, they found a house of sorts. Soon Jack had four half-siblings and a new surname.

John Verdun Smith-Deragon had very little formal schooling. He never finished high-school due to the Great Depression and subsequent family unravellings. Jessie's government pension covering the loss of his father stopped when he turned sixteen so he had to start fending. It was bootstrap time.

Fortunately, Jack was a reader and a dreamer and, of necessity, sometimes a schemer. These traits, plus his love of writing, would serve him well. I doubt any high school drop-out of today would be able to do as well as he did.

At the age of sixteen he returned to Toronto.

I explored Union Station thoroughly; got a part-time job washing dishes on a dining-car. Little glamour to this. I became a news agent which is sort of pimping for Planters' Peanuts and Sweet-Marie bars. It was tough. Consider: my first day's pay grossed 90 cents, of which 18 cents was mine. I learned the trick was to carry half your own stock, purchased through a fence for stolen goods, or re-selling newspapers. I once sold the Toronto Telegram four times on the way to London.

In his spare time Jack knocked on doors.

One door led to the Family Herald where a W.T. Murchie, circulation manager, said, "You look too young, Kid. What makes you think you can sell?"
"I'm hungry."
He assigned me to Jack Gould's crew and wished me luck. I thanked him and used his phone to quit being a news agent.

Through guile and charm Jack managed to sell an impressive number of subscriptions around the countryside. Sometimes he netted himself $17 in one day. For the next two weeks he did well, making sales and becoming a bit cocky. It didn't last.

Inevitably I hit a dry spell... Now what? I was hungry and sorry for myself. For the first time in my life, I realised that I could fall over dead in the ditch and no one would care. The sky would remain blue, the bird-song would be sweet and the green grass would darken not a whit. Whether I ate or not was entirely my problem. Root, hog----or die!

He survived, of course. Sometimes he slept rough in train stations. He spent some time in jail too, in a case of mistaken identity.
Gould has been bitching about the Essex Super-Six and now we drive in a Studebaker President Eight. It is a monster of a car; black with maroon trim, a seven passenger with folding jump seats in the back. The hood is as long as forever because not

only is this an Eight, it is a Straight Eight and each cylinder is the diameter of a wine jug. It eats gas, but that's only about 20 cents a gallon.

THESE ARE THE THINGS I'VE LEARNED:

If farmers don't have money, try for eggs.

No eggs? Try for chickens…what the hell, they're not laying…

No chickens? Try for gold…any gold fillings fall out of your tooth? Sure, I'll give you a four-year subscription for that…

Gould taught me how to recognise good gold pieces. Then a bit about old art prints; how to spot Currier and Ives originals, of which there were a lot in the country back then. We'd deal for anything and by the end of the week the old President Eight often looked like a gypsy caravan until we off-loaded eggs and chickens. Every major center had a Swift's or Canada Packers that bought eggs and chickens.

Hooked rugs were worth picking up too. Quilts. Army stuff, but not the Great War helmets, had to be older, back to the Boer War or the Fenian Raids or the Northwest Rebellions (Riel). And Gould liked contemporary stuff too. He picked up two .38 revolvers (with ammunition) which he kept stowed in his bag. Nervous-making because he already had an army pistol from his days in The Royal Canadian Horse Artillery at Kingston.

A month on the road…time to check into Toronto. Our picture has been in The Family Herald as the highest producing subscription crew. High spirits! Down Highway 15 to Kingston, up Princess Street, *where Gould unfortunately makes a left turn on Wellington. Whistle! Gould's license has expired. Cop looks over three characters in a big black sedan and I suppose he's been seeing Jimmy Cagney movies. Down to the police station and we're all inside. Questioning. I'm guessing what's going on inside the car. Bingo!*

They find three pistols. They find one of us traveling under an alias; Bert Carr is really Alberto Arcari. A-hah! I give Gould credit though; he's quick to defend us, to say the guns were his alone. Great! The cops would just check in W.T. Murchie in Toronto to be sure we were what we claimed to be. Meanwhile Jack Gould entered the slammer. Bert and I were told not to leave town. Toronto office vouched for us next morning and Gould was free to go...after he paid the fine for having three unregistered weapons, now confiscated, and an out-dated driver's license. This took all our money. We left town broke.

Monday morning, we headed west on concession roads, selling like mad for whatever we could get. We were desperate and had a hell of a good week. By Friday we had made up our losses and headed west on Highway 2. Into Oshawa...through Oshawa...suddenly a motorcycle cop is on our tail, then, magically, two cops. Into Whitby and we are stopped on Main Street.

We are arrested for armed robbery in Odessa on Saturday night. Off directly to jail. We are place in separate cells. No talking. A disappointing evening.

Two detectives pick us up next morning and take us back to Napanee, handcuffed together. A third de-

tective drives our car back, at our expense. The drive is long enough for conversation with the detectives, who are not bad fellows. When we learn the details of our alleged crime, we know we have a proper answer to that. We had stayed with a family named Parrot that night, Mr. Parrot arrives in Napanee and identifies us. We're clear.

Except: It's Saturday afternoon. The judge is away for the long weekend. So...enjoy!

Late Monday afternoon we are released. Finally, we get to Toronto. Bert goes home. We never see him again.

Jack carried on selling for The Family Herald, got approval to form his own crew, bought his own car, a 1927 Star and tried once more to make something happen with Bella. She told him she was too old for him. Six months older---how could that be too old? He took that to mean, "Get lost!" And so, he did."

He got lost again up in Jellicoe, having heard about a gold-rush going on there. No gold, but he stayed for a few months working as a sign-painter. He also fulfilled a long-standing goal. He lost his virginity.

I got to know a very nice girl who waited tables at the hotel. She gave me special portions. She relieved my worries by teaching me with great care how boys get rid of this virginity thing. I wasn't very good at it (her words), at first, but I persisted.

The following spring Jack moved to Ste. Hyacinthe, Quebec, and briefly joined his family, now minus stepfather Albert who had wandered off like so many men did during the Depression. He got a job at the local canning factory and set himself up in a boarding house, then an apartment, shared with another young man, Doug, who became a life-long friend.

Jack and Doug, young, handsome, eligible Anglos in a large French community made the most of their status and learned enough French to be able to get friendly with the likes of Yvonne, Claire, Laurette and Lucie.

One spring night her sister arrived early. Doug wasn't home. She explained that they wouldn't be coming by any more. Yvonne was getting married and it wouldn't look right. I agreed. However, she thought the occasion rated a proper adieu, and, why not me? Why not indeed? And so we said our adieus, until six o'clock, when she said, "Dites bonjour a Doug pour moi."

"Avec plaisir," I replied.

The Canning Factory: *The work day is ten hours. There are no paid holidays but if Christmas or Dominion Day falls on a work day you can take the day off---without pay. No overtime, no health plan, no accident plan. I invented a bean-snipper, sure it would make my fortune. It worked well. It snipped off the tip of my right distal finger with no trouble at all. Very painful. No workman's compensation.*

In his spare time Jack wrote stories for railroad magazines and other publications. A few years later one of his stories was noticed by the director of National Business Publications Ltd. in Ste. Anne de Bellevue, Quebec. He offered Jack a position there as junior editor of one of their industrial magazines. As they say, follow your bliss. It will take you there, eventually. Or close.

Chapter 13
Phyllis

In Ste. Hyacinthe Jack met Phyllis, my mother. They discovered things they had in common: they both lacked active fathers and they had both, by necessity, quit school to help out the family by working wherever they could. While Jack was canning peas, Phyllis worked as a stocking-topper for Gotham Gold Stripe. Her job was to finish the tops of the silk/nylon stockings women wore with the help of a garter belt. The blessed invention of pantyhose was still years away.

Phyllis was fluently bilingual. Her mother and grandmother were French Protestant, a minority in Quebec. Children in this minority attended English school but elsewhere French was the spoken language. Jack picked up enough Joual to get along at the canning factory. Oddly, his confreres asked him to speak English to them. "We have to learn your language. You don't need to learn ours." (How things have changed!)

Jack: " *It's terrible but I don't remember our first date. We just sort of drifted into friendship. Phyllis lived on Bernier Street with her grandmother and younger sister. I began showing up, bringing chocolate-covered cherries in a brown paper bag. Often while Phyllis was getting ready Memere and I would eat all the chocolates.*

There are no photos of their wedding day. The

person in charge had neglected to put film in his camera. They were married in a little Anglican church on Thanksgiving weekend. The church was decorated with pumpkins, apples and corn stocks. One of the local guests asked if this was a wedding tradition in Protestant churches. Mon Onc' Etienne explained that, yes, it was done to symbolise a fruitful marriage.

Jack and Phyllis were in their early twenties when Lorna Mae was born. She lived for ten days. Spina bifida.

Jack: *"The doctor made me look at her back so I would know. She had such a beautiful face. Her back had a three-inch hole revealing exposed vertebrae and ganglia. There was no hope. Your mother and I fell into a form of catatonic despair. The news about the Germans smashing Belgrade or the suicide by drowning of Virginia Wolfe held no interest for me."*

I believe the death of their first-born marked their marriage beyond suffering. Jack thought he was being kind by taking care of the funeral himself and keeping Phyllis away. She later told me that she had always resented that, but, as was her way, she kept it to herself.

Jack's new job took them to Ste. Anne de Bellevue. It must have been a welcome distraction as well as an improved income. They rented a two-storey brick house at the top of the hill, right in the center of the village. From Lamarche Street west most residents are Francophone and live on narrow streets called St. Pierre, Legault and St. Joseph. East of Lamarche the streets get wider and most residents are Anglo. Macdonald College campus marks the eastern border of the town. It provides beautiful green space with specimen trees and orchards. The Ottawa River meets the St. Lawrence River a few miles east of the college.

Two years after Lorna Mae died, almost to the day, I was born, right in the middle of a March snowstorm and World War Two. I was a War Baby, in the vanguard of the Baby Boomers. I have early memories of being wheeled in my pram to the college campus and of being able to run free across the wide grassy spaces across from the orange brick faculty buildings with their terra cotta tiled rooftops.

Jack enjoyed his new position in the publishing business. He was able to use his writing skills, albeit in an industrial capacity. It wasn't romantic stuff but it paid well and he could always write his novels later.

He also decided that it would be a good idea to volunteer in the Canadian Armed Forces.

Chapter 14
Jack's War

As well as his army pay, Jack received his regular salary from National Business Publications, a very generous arrangement indeed. Originally trained in the artillery Jack managed to put his writing skills to good use and was soon seconded to the British Forces Network. His job was ideal for his talents. He wrote scripts and prepared musical entertainment as well as human-interest stories gleaned from what he saw and heard. He rode in a mobile van around England and Holland with his crew, broadcasting morale-boosting radio programs. Some of these went to Canada as well. Whenever possible he would write himself into the script of a play, entitling him to more pay.

He had a typewriter that he named Betsy Ann and on it he typed airmail letters to Phyllis, almost every day. She kept them and now I have them, stored in their original leather box. They tell of a very homesick young man having the occasional lark out with the boys. He was handsome, had a bit of a Tyrone Power look. Women today remark that he resembled George Clooney. He was also a natural mimic so his letters took on a rather British tone.

London, November 4, 1944
Phyl, my dear,
You know, darling, these English do know how to live and enjoy themselves. There's a sort of ease

and unconscious refinement about their theatres and bars and hotels; about their manner and way of speaking, of entertaining that's truly remarkable... and I don't for a moment forget what a fortunate guy I am to be in a position where I can see the better side of life here...

London, November 16, 1944

Phyl darling,

Got a confession to make! Got a bit squiffed last night but I feel fine today nonetheless...

London, November 18, 1944

Phyl darling,

I feel badly because I missed writing you yesterday. But the way things turned out I missed a lot of things. Everything started out innocently: Capt. Kesten was going out of town to a certain supply depot to get some equipment for the mobile unit. He buzzed into the office and asked if I'd like to come along. Being caught up in my work I said sure. So away we drove, with Valentine and another chap. Our schedule called for us to be back by three---but then trouble cropped up. On the way back we got lost and by the time we found the road again it was getting dark. We had many, many miles to cover and time was getting short. We each had a broadcast to do so there we were, really clipping along in the little Hillman. And then---bing! Our spotlight went out and we were completely in the dark. We managed to get it fixed and roared on over the slippery wet pavement. We reached the outskirts of London bomb-al-

ley when an alert sounded so we had to douse the spotlight. We skittered across the black streets like a scalded cat, one eye on the road, one eye on our watches. We had eighteen minutes to get back to Oxford Street Studio but suddenly the old car just sort of phut-t-ted and died. We were out of petrol. So we were really hung up...stranded. Missed the broadcast and everything else. So this morning we are getting a lot of ribbing because missing a broadcast is simply NOT DONE.

Most of these letters were typed on blue airmail paper. It is amazing how few typos he made. No spell-check on that old Underwood. One day Jack and his buddy Valentine got their jeep caught up in the Arnhem Bridge that had been partly blown up. The impact gave Jack a split nose and a banged-up knee. Betsy Ann, his Underwood, tumbled out and splashed into the Maas River. That was probably the worst of his physical injuries during his war experience. But he did witness some horrible things. The following excerpts are from his clandestine war diary, an artefact now in my possession.

February, 1945
...thundering down the runway---England drops below us at a startling rate; now here we are, 20 men and equipment droning 1500 feet above the English landscape. Fascinating.
There are 3 parachutes. But there are plenty of little waxed paper bags: Bags, paper, vomiting, other ranks for use of...

And the coastline slips beneath our wings. On our port side are the cliffs of Dover.

<u>Nine Minutes</u>

And there is the coast of France and the beaches of Normandy. A flotilla of LCTs-about 25-cruise along near the shore. We pass the beaches, inland, over a panorama of old desolation, destruction and the green festering wounds of the shell craters filled with stagnant water.

Fighter planes dip and wheel about.

The ground seems to rush up at a terrific speed and you realise you are coming in for a landing.

Drove through seas of mud---took a guy to check for mines around our site. Entered the woods cautiously. Old German dugouts. Well battered. Horrible stench. Got worse. We found him under some pine shrubs. His head was several feet away. His two mates were all in one piece but very dead. They swell up. They were buried in their own slit-trenches. Mac said, "Here, you sons-of-bitches, better keep these with you." and tossed in a couple of broken rifles. They landed with a dullish thud. Then they were covered. Crossed sticks were set up and to the crossbar we hung three German helmets. We were silent for a moment, then Mac said, as we walked away, "Puir bastards." I knew exactly what he meant.

In the Night is the title of a song Dad wrote during his days in Ste. Hyacinthe, presumably after meeting my mother. It's a romantic ballad filled with the idealism of young love. Now in Hamburg near the end of the war, Dad had the opportunity to have his song recorded. It was to be accompanied by Gerhardt Gregor on the marvellous organ in the studio of Radio Hamburg. The vocal would be sung by Dad's friend, Bill Valentine. However…

Phyl Darling,

Well, yesterday was quite a day…or evening. Bill and I went down to the Ship and Dragon and our man had our table reserved and we had a very nice dinner and he brought us a bottle of Champagne, which we drank. Then he brought us another bottle which we put under the table. A little while later he confided that he could get us still another bottle, and this is very fine indeed, and so there we are, having three sparkling bottles of Champagne and we are feeling quite good, so we top it off with a Scotch, each. Then off we go on our merry way to the recording studio. Now we realise we are both high as kites and we can't find our jeep. Nevertheless, we totter over to Radio Hamburg where Gerhardt is waiting at the organ. Well, poor old Bill had to concentrate too much on standing and he couldn't concentrate on the song so well and it is slightly loused up in the recording. But the organ part! Absolutely terrific! We recorded it on tape and made a dubbing onto a disc…

I remember listening to that disc as a child. The strange thing was that to play it on a turntable the stylus arm had to be placed at what we would consider the end of the record. Somehow it worked and indeed, the organ part was impressive.

As the war was winding down Jack was offered the opportunity to stay in England and continue working with the British Forces Network, writing radio scripts. He was tempted but felt he should stay loyal to National Business Publications. Also, he didn't think Phyllis would be happy away from her familiar surroundings. Another factor had to do with a young woman he had met in Hamburg. Helga and he had become close, just how close I don't really know, but he did remark several times that he wouldn't have wanted Helga and Phyllis to meet.

His decision not to stay on in England would become one of his later "what ifs?"

If he had stayed, I would have developed a British accent. I was two and a half when he returned to Canada and I have a hazy memory of that time. Mom had gone to Montreal to meet the troop train, accompanied by her brother, my Uncle Lorne, who was home from his navy tour. Maybe she needed moral support but when she met Jack at the station poor Lorne was dismissed rather quickly. Of course, I don't remember that encounter but I do have mind pictures of the following evening. It was a party, our house was filled with friends and family, lots of noise and music and Mom in an elegant black dress. The dress had black netting at the top of the bodice. It had black sequins sewn in a leafy pattern. Her shoes were black suede with ankle-straps. But I have no memory of my father that night. He was just another soldier in uniform.

Chapter 15
A Couple of Glitches

I finish dictating Chapter One of Land of Triangles and drop it off at The Lodge for Dad to listen to through the headphones. When I return home the phone is already ringing.

"Just a suggestion; could you read a bit more slowly next time? I'm having trouble catching every word. It's very good though, you speak clearly, just a touch too quickly." I agree to comply. Chapter Two will sound as though Margaret Atwood is reading it. I drone away but find it's difficult to speak at half-speed. I'm not a speed-talker like so many young people today but I guess we all have our own comfortable pace.

The next day I deliver Chapter Two and pick up the recorder with Chapter One. Back home I get ready to dictate Chapter Three. I make a discovery. I break up laughing as I play back the first chapter. I sound like The Chipmunks! Then I notice the switch on the side of the machine. It's a speed-altering switch and it's been set at 'high'. I had told my father not to fiddle with the buttons on the right side. "Just push the 'play' and 'stop' buttons on the left." But Dad has always been a fiddler and pays little attention to rules. Well, now I know I can continue reading at my usual pace.

Uh-oh! A bit of a hiccup here! Nurse Lizzie has called from The Lodge. She *is* a speed-talker but

I manage to make out the important words; Jack! Ambulance! Hospital! I'm not really surprised. The night before I'd been chatting with Dad on the phone and he'd sounded weird, having trouble finding the right words, calling his wheelchair his highchair, things like that. He told me he felt as if his head was in another part of the room, laughing at his body.

I called the hospital and asked the nurse in the E.R. what she could tell me about my father.

"Well," she said, "your father is a very nice man."

"Thank you. I think so too. And... apart from that?"

It turned out to be a 'touch of pneumonia' and they sent him home by ambulance that night. When I saw him the next day he was dressed and looking just fine. But now I'm thinking I'd better get cracking on this project...maybe we don't have all the time in the world. Last week his parking permit for disabled people was renewed. The expiry date is November 2016. I mentioned this to him and told him we had another five years to work on his stories. He thought that sounded reasonable. "Then I'll be one hundred and then I can die!" Because in his mind this is only the beginning. You have to love that kind of optimism.

And yet...

Chapter 16
Tombstone

In an excerpt from Land of Triangles Jack writes: *...and like many men of his age, he had no one with whom he could talk about the things that keep a man awake at three a.m.: things like the eternal consternation about dying---the shrinking capacity to enjoy life---the soul-shrivelling realisation there are no finite limits to potential.*

I must remember that Dad was much younger when he wrote those words and they were meant to be the thoughts of an even younger man, Jonathan, who was in his mid-forties. Dad had always worried about dying, not the actual act, of course, but the things he would miss out on. He loves to plan, to try to control his future as best he can. His funeral is prepaid. Thanks, Dad. Nothing is left to chance. Recently he handed me an envelope, sealed and marked To Be Opened After My Death. Then he asked me to open it. "But Dad, you're not...". "Never mind, just open it. I want to go over things with you first."

He has indicated which music is to be played at his service, what newspapers to contact for his obit, who is invited to come back to the house (my house, I suppose) afterwards as well as suggestions for the food and drinks table. There will be no surprises. The tombstone is already in place with Mom's urn beneath it. Dad and I designed it six years ago while we sat in the showroom of Martel

Monuments. We had already decided on some trailing ivy around Mom's name to honour her love of gardening. Now Dad asked, "Do you think a locomotive engine would be in bad taste?" Considering his passion for trains and that he always sketched a locomotive engine on the flyleaf of his books I replied," Why not?" We paged through the catalogue and indeed found a charming template of an engine belching smoke. The tombstone was made to order and is, I believe, the most unique of all the markers in the Barb Road Cemetery.

Mom and Dad used to argue, jokingly but not really, about who would die first. Neither one wanted to be left behind. The day we took her to the hospital they were still bickering about it in a jesting way to cover their fear. I think Mom realised she had won that argument. She died six weeks later. After her service Dad was lost. He told me how they had become closer during the last few years at The Lodge, how they would lie together on the bed and talk about the early past. And the past was all Mom had and perhaps her memory loss allowed her to forget some of her earlier unexpressed resentment towards him. It seems their married intimacy was book-ended.

But Dad is still here and so for the past six years I have listened, over and over, to his tales of his lowly beginnings, his successes, his disappointments, his mistakes and, of course, his women. He loves to talk about his women.

Why do men chase women?
Because they fear death.
(from the film Moonstruck)

Chapter 17
Helga

There is a picture of her in Jack's war diary. <u>That</u> Helga. She is blonde, young, innocent- looking. He stayed for a while with her family in Hamburg as the war was winding down. He was impressed with their hospitality and has more than once described the first meal he was served. It was a platter of cold sliced meat, decorated with a border of fresh dark purple pansies. He understood that despite food shortages these people carried on with no lack of grace. On the last page of his diary he wrote this poem.

Hob-nailed feet, steady beat,
Searing burning intolerable heat-
Choking maddening clouds of dust,
You want to stop,
You go on, you must.
Left- right, left-right
(I left you, right? I left you right.)

And so Helga makes an appearance in Land of Triangles but she is Helga in name only. *Helga, a big woman, an explosive personality with a great zest for good food and gaiety. Her hair is raven black and shimmers with remarkable highlights. Her dark eyes burn and crackle with life. She is a mixture of Magyar, German and Gypsy, which is as close as one can get to being a true Hungarian.*

It turns out that Helga and Kate have been enjoying a lesbian relationship. Perhaps in this fiction Jack (Jonathan) can rationalise Bella's (Kate's) earlier rejection of him in Kingston.

Chapter 18
The Villain

Yesterday when I visited him Dad handed me a notepad and asked me to write down the names of all the characters in his manuscript. We're now on chapter twelve of his manuscript review but I'm afraid all I'm accomplishing is to entertain my father for a few hours as he listens to my recorded readings of his novel. This is not a bad thing, I suppose. He can't remember the names of his characters. It doesn't help that he has changed them along the way, from re-write to re-write. In one paragraph Jonathan Wade became Jamieson Slade, then back again. But the one character he always remembers is Luke Pooney. That name never changes. He is the villain.

Luke stalks people on the trails around Hector, not with evil intent but just to find out what they do. The object is to see without being seen---not that easy because Luke is an awkward boy with a large head and a shock of yellow hair.

Luke Pooney...what a dreadful name! And an equally despicable character as it turns out. I wonder why, then, he is one of the most believable ones. Jonathan, the protagonist, is less well-drawn. Jonathan, the sensitive navel-gazer, has no face. We learn that Kate has brown eyes with greenish glints and that she doesn't shrink from profanities. Amanda has violet eyes and is a sharp dresser and businesswoman. Even Helga, who has only a bit part, is clearly described. I guess it's difficult to paint one's own portrait.

There have been a few villains in my father's life but none were more of a torment than the one he never knew. Or, if he did know him, he couldn't be sure it *was* him. But he'll never know for sure because that secret died with my mother. She fell in love with him, whoever he was. She was young and foolish, certainly foolish enough to confess her feelings to Dad. I was eight years old at the time, blissfully unaware of the emotional drama taking place around me.

Our summers in those days were spent at my grandparents' house in Elmira, Ontario, a good twelve hour drive from our home in Ste. Annes. This was before the Macdonald-Cartier Freeway was built. The 401. Sometimes we took the train. I remember our first overnight journey in a roomette, me on the top bunk and baby sister Lynne in a basket down below with Mom and Dad. In the morning we had breakfast by the window, watching the passing landscape, cows in the fields dotted yellow with dandelions, farm houses in the distance, other trains whizzing past the other way.

Mom's parents had reunited shortly after the end of the war. It was not a blissful reunion; Papoe had an insouciant weirdness about him. He didn't give a damn how others saw him but he did have a practical side. He realised the home Dad had returned to after the war was too crowded. My grandmother, Mamoe, spent a lot of time there as well as her daughter, Doris, her son, Lorne and her own mother, Memere, my great grandmother. Papoe had found work in Elmira as an electrician at Naugatuck Chemicals and had bought a house. So, he ordered his family, including Memere, to move in with him. That's how our summers in Elmira began. I loved it there. I soon found a small gang of kids my age to play with and the best thing was the new swimming pool where I learned to swim very well.

Dad stayed behind in Ste. Annes to work but always took a week off to visit us. He would drive, sometimes in a rented car, sometimes on the train. That summer when I was eight Dad came for his visit and, as he told me recently, Mom told him she was in love with another man. It was an inevitable situation, really. Here she was, young, attractive, charming and with her extended family around to look after Lynne and me. And her husband was away.

Dad: "If only she hadn't confessed! But no, she had to blurt it all out almost as soon as I had arrived! In love, for Christ's sake! What was I supposed to do?"

Me: "So, what did you do?"

Dad: "I told her that if she wanted to go away with this guy and find out whether she was truly in love with him I wouldn't stand in her way. I told her to take a week, a month, whatever she needed. But, of course, there was you and Lynne to consider. I suggested we each take one of you. Naturally that didn't go down well, not with me either."

Me: " So you gave her no choice, really."

Dad: "Well, no...I knew she wouldn't leave you two. So, I suggested she have a long talk with this bastard, whoever he was, and then make her decision. She arranged to meet him in Waterloo. I drove her there and left her near some undisclosed location. I went to see a movie. No idea what movie it was. Then I picked her up. She was crying but never said another word about it. I left her at your grandparents' house and drove all the way back to Ste. Annes the same night in a furious rage. She took the train home the next night. We never discussed it again. Never."

Me: "I do remember that train trip home. Mom, Lynne and I sharing a berth...it was crowded. I didn't understand why we were leaving Elmira so early. I find it sad that you and Mom couldn't talk about it. I know Mom was good at keeping secrets. For all her liberal attitudes she was very concerned about appearances."

Dad: "You know, we never really talked all that much, not about feelings. I tried once in a while to have intimate conversations with her but there was always a barrier."

Me: "I felt that barrier too. Sometimes I was afraid to be alone with Mom in case that wall came between us. Or maybe I put up my own wall. Lynne was better at talking the heavy stuff with her. I always felt more comfortable opening up to you, Dad."

Dad: "Well, I'm happy for that. But dammit! I still don't know who that bastard was."

Me: "Does it really matter now?"

Dad: "When you get as old and decrepit as I am

there's not much else to do except think about old stuff. It's crazy, I know."

Me: "Dad, I wish you could live more in the present but I get that for you the present sucks. And the future...well, I guess that sucks even more."

Yes, to him it mattered. We always want to know who the villain was. But the double standard ruled in those days. Dad could have his liaisons and not feel the need to unburden himself; he felt no guilt because in his mind Mom was always number one. And besides, she never questioned him. I think she felt relief that Dad had other women in his life. Strange?

In all good stories the villain finally gets what's coming. Luke Pooney was no exception.

Luke's first shot hit behind my right shoulder, shattering a corner of my scapula. The bullet went right through me and lodged in Kate's upper right arm. The second shot was lower and did the greatest damage: it deflected off the ilium, clipped a corner of the ascending colon and just missed the liver and kidney. It stayed inside me.

I never heard the third shot. Shock left us inert. I'm sure Luke presumed us dead before he placed the muzzle under his chin.

Chapter 19
Party On

They were a good-looking couple, Jack with his devilish blue-green eyes that crinkled at the corners, Phyllis with her dark wavy hair and fine figure. In their early thirties they had lots of friends and it was often party time. Ste. Annes is a small town that then had easy access to buses, trains and taxis for those who lived farther away but most friends were within walking distance so party time was safer. Also, fewer people drove cars so drinking and driving were not an issue. Jack liked to be the life of these parties. At the least opportunity he would whip out his harmonica or strum along on Mabel, his mandolin. He enjoyed his drinks, usually beer in those days, sometimes a few too many which made him expansive or sentimental. Phyllis sipped at her drinks. When the parties were at our house Lynne and I would watch the goings-on from our upstairs vantage point, the grate in the floor that looked down on the kitchen. Sometimes we sent notes through the grate, attached to string, requesting favours. *Please come upstairs with some chips and ginger ale.* Usually some happy guest would trot upstairs and oblige us.

We had a player-piano in the dining-room so things often got noisy. Uncle Don played popular jazz/swing numbers quite well and he often got carried away with mirthful renditions of Sentimental Journey or Firefly. One of the piano rolls was the

William Tell Overture, always good for a laugh when some guest decided it would be fun to pump away at breakneck speed. We also had a record player that stacked the discs for added musical ambiance.

Often parties at our house involved plays that Dad had written with parts for each guest to read aloud into the disc-recorder mic. The plays were light and silly and fun for Lynne and me to replay the next morning. The lobster party night was one I remember for the blood-curdling screams the guests emitted as the lobsters were dropped into the boiling water.

I loved it when the house was full of people, especially when they were Mom's relatives whose French and English flowed and intermingled effortlessly. Mon Onc' Etienne often told jokes in his booming voice. He would start in English but when the punch line came it was always delivered in French. For some reason it was funnier that way. I was soon motivated to understand French. I wanted to get the jokes.

But when everyone left and we were just the four of us I sometimes felt an uneasy tension, an invisible curtain between Mom and Dad. It made me sad.

Chapter 20
New Gadgets

We read to know we are not alone. How does a man feel less alone when he can no longer read?
. . . C.S. Lewis

Manon, the rep from the CNIB, is visiting Dad at The Lodge this morning. I join them and help get Dad familiar with two new devices; a cc t.v. magnifying screen and a talking-book player. The magnifier has one power switch and three knobs for adjusting font size. Dad is thrilled to be able finally to see his words in print again even if they are enlarged to such a size that he can read only three words at a time. He asks Manon, "What do you think of an old fart like me trying to write a book?" She replies," I think it's wonderful when people want to keep on trying. These are the ones we are so happy to help."

The disc player has more knobs and though simple to operate I have a feeling it will be problematic. The novel Manon leaves on the player is Paris 1919 by Margaret McMillan. I know Dad read it eight years ago but he doesn't remember. Right now, he is only focused on one thing. His manuscript. I also know I will be getting a lot of phone calls from him over the next few days.

The first one comes as soon as I get home. He has forgotten where the power switch is. The next call comes later that evening. He is gasping from the effort of dialling out. It has taken him an hour to reach me so I remind him that he doesn't need to press 1, we're not long distance. (Lynne is though, so press 1 for her.) And now he has forgotten why he called so he asks, "What's new?" I tell him, "We're having problems with the pump for the well and had to get a plumber and it's still not fixed. We can't flush the toilet unless George primes the pump by hand." Oh, good!", he replies. I don't bother to reconstruct this situation in his mind so that he could make a more appropriate remark. Our plumbing problem doesn't affect him. There was a time when he would have come right over to offer his help. Those days are long gone.

The new gadgets are not going to prove very helpful. I need to think of something else to distract Dad. He's becoming shirty about the delay in his book becoming published. He continues to talk about the Christmas book market. Well, we're now into October, the weather is still warm and as I cast about for a solution to my ongoing dilemma of trying to keep Dad happy while deceiving him about the status of his book I come up with a good distraction.

Chapter 21
His Last Train Ride

Lynne and Frank have just moved to a townhouse in Guildwood. There is a VIA train station nearby. Dad loves the train and hasn't seen his other daughter for a while. I book our tickets, assigned seats from Cornwall to Guildwood, return. Dad is excited and packed, ready for our little trip. My big concern is how to get Dad up on the train and to his seat without mishap. He is so unsteady on his feet but he does use a cane. At the station I take him to the washroom door and hope he actually pees before we board the train. The next hurdle is negotiating him up the steps to the coach. A burly assistant helps. Good. Now to find our assigned seats. Disaster! The coach is filled with Japanese tourists. Our seats are taken. I desperately look for an assistant while trying to prop up my father who is cursing at the tourists who just sit and grin as we lurch down the aisle. The assistant finally finds us a seat and apologises, explaining that these tourists will be getting off at Kingston. So much for assigned seats.

Dad looks disgruntled. "Yes, Dad, I know train travel was better in your day. Yes, I know about the dining cars with white linen tablecloths. It was nice, wasn't it?" Dad decides to have a snooze and indeed the tourists disembark at Kingston. A few hours after that we pull in to Guildwood Station. And now a new hurdle. The elevator isn't working so we must stagger down a flight of stairs. Fuck!

Lynne and Frank come to our rescue as we make our wobbly descent and finally reach their car. Once inside the front seat Dad forgets his recent discomforts because this car is no ordinary car. No, it's a big boat of a 1983 Toronado, once owned by Gordon Lightfoot. Frank, a big fan of Lightfoot, bought it on a whim. Dad is suitably impressed. We drive on to their new home and a new problem presents itself. Stairs. This townhouse has four flights of stairs including the basement. Dad's bedroom is on the second floor. I get the couch in the basement where the huge TV. is set up. We spend the afternoon chatting in the living room and after dinner it's TV downstairs. Dad opts to go to bed early rather than brave the trip down, then up two flights of stairs to his sleeping quarters.

Besides, he must be tired from the excitement of the day.

The next day offers more excitement. Frank has offered to take Dad for a drive down memory lane. He knows Toronto very well and Dad has so many memories of places where he and his mother resided when he was a young lad called Jackie Smith.

After lunch we all pile into the Toronado---Dad in the front with Frank. Dad is in heaven, being chauffeured around in the generously appointed front seat. I am in the back between Lynne and her daughter Melissa. Not much to see from there---the side windows are rather small. But never mind. This is all about showing Dad a good time.

Eventually we turn onto Ontario Street, find the number of the rowhouse and park for a bit outside.

Dad never lived there but his mother and her other children did. I remember visiting there as a very young child. There was a beautiful pair of doors to the living room with etched glass panels that fascinated me.

On we go to Church Street. Oops, that house is gone. Reverse to Charles Street, yes, that might be the place, now on to Dovercourt Road, pull a u-ey, something familiar there? Frank is a good and patient driver, enjoying this as much as Dad is. I can see very little, of course, but so what? After another hour of prowling the streets of old Toronto we turn onto Queen and find a restaurant. There is always a restaurant at the end of a journey. It's a little bistro with good bread and wine. When we leave I notice Dad clutching a small bag. It's his dessert, a cherry pie to eat on the way home. The pie is finished before we reach the 401. Dad opens his window and tosses the bag. "Litterbug!", we all yell from the back seat. I worry about us being arrested and say so. Dad is from a different time and besides, he could always justify littering. "The pigeons will take care of it."

Our sojourn over we exit the Toronado and relax in the living room, Dad recounting some of the recent sightings of old familiar haunts. He falls asleep easily on the sofa with a smile on his face. Two days later we get back on the train. No glitches this time and I remember very little of the ride home. Dad dozed for most of the journey. There was no mention of his manuscript. A satisfactory result.

Chapter 22
Northern Bliss

"Who wants to come to Jellicoe with me?"

Dad would ask that question to friends and family from time to time, more often getting a resounding "NO!". But occasionally someone would agree and before they could change their mind the car was packed and off they would go in a cloud of dust, heading for my father's magnetic north, Lake Superior and beyond. A trip to Jellicoe wasn't just a quick nip down the 401, no; it was a shun-pike journey over secondary roads, two days of driving past nothing more exciting than the Wawa Goose or the Albino Moose, followed by endless miles of evergreens and hydro poles. At last, you would reach that magical destination, that legendary Eden which has lived on in my father's mind as pure heaven. You might be a bit disappointed. There is nothing there.

I must admit my only close encounter with the place was a five-minute photo-op. I was crotch-deep in snow hanging on to the sign that read Jellicoe on the edge of the Trans Canada Highway. (My husband, George, and I were on our way to the west coast, idiotically enough, in February. We had to prove to my father that we had indeed taken that route but we refrained from further exploration. It was minus thirty-five degrees.) But those who have made the actual visit will tell you the same thing. There is nothing there. My mother, grandmother, brother-in-law and my youngest son, Andrew, have all experienced the nothingness of the place. They related how Dad would drive them to a location by an empty field and point to a tree. "Next to that tree was our house!" Or they would find themselves standing near a swampy inlet of a lake and learn, "That's where I almost drowned!" Photographs would be taken and later compared with older sepia-toned images of the same barren locations taken during the thirties.

Back then Jellicoe was a railroad divisional point. Jack's stepfather was in charge of a section of railway telegraph lines and not much else. There was a rail yard, a round house and a hotel. No stores, no schools or churches or hospitals. It did have clean lakes, good fishing and hunting. Today these virtues are touted by local entrepreneurs. Originally called Hector in 1916 it was renamed Jellicoe after a British Admiral. (Place names in Upper Canada tend to honour conflict and its leaders: Waterloo, Kitchener, Brantford, Brockville, Wellington, Kingston, Simcoe. In Lower Canada it's the saints and their miracles; Sainte Anne de Bellevue, Sainte Anne de Beaupre, Saint Eustache, Saint Simeon.)

Excerpt from Land of Triangles:
I learned there was no high school in Hector and I would be obliged to travel daily up to Orient Lake. Kate explained train schedules and the joys of commuting to school on freight trains and locals, riding in cabooses and baggage cars. "And apart from that... what does anybody do in Hector?" "Winter we skate

and go tobogganing. I run a rabbit trap-line and read and play records. And there's homework. A lot of men play poker and drink. That's about it."

Despite its desolation Jack became enchanted by the place. He was in his early teens, an impressionable age. His two big obsessions began there: locomotives and Bella M. None of his half-siblings have such passion for Jellicoe and have often wondered why Jack is so besotted with it. They were much younger and shared only half his gene-pool. Their experience of it was not the same.

From Land of Triangles a.k.a. Trainwatchers, with revised time-frame:

In this third year of our twenty first century, Katherine Willison is still a woman of sleek mystery. My strange love for her began in 1964. It is an unrequited relationship of no current validity.

I tell myself that Katherine no longer fits our hard Shield country. She's grown beyond the hard discipline of our ancient rocks and the Redwater system that forms the aorta of our world. It has nothing to do with the killing of her father.

Chapter 23
Raisins and the Male Cook

I can't help thinking of that "Down the Mines" skit from Beyond the Fringe, the line that goes something like, "Not much conversation here, down the mines. Barely enough to keep the mind alive." It's a bit like that here at The Lodge, as I suppose it is at any similar facility. Mealtimes are eerily silent. No chatter, no laughter. It must have to do with hearing impairments or the scarcity of common interests or depression. My father usually spends a couple of minutes at his assigned table, eats a few mouthfuls, then quickly wheels himself back to the refuge of his room where he can forage through his little fridge for something more exciting. Ham and cheese on raisin bread is always nice. Chocolate-covered cherries or ice cream bars are wonderful. I shop for him to make sure he has these treats always on hand. His large screen TV. is his usual dining company though he always switches it off when I arrive.

Today I am impressed to find him dressed and alert and sitting at his desk. His desk is pristine, save for the new magnifier and some papers. I don't ask what he has done with the litter of unrelated artefacts that usually live on his desk top. Most of the time he is semi-prone in his lounger, watching TV or dozing with his back to the door. He often doesn't hear a knock at the door because of the TV blare. Once he *did* hear me knock and leaned back so far that he tipped over and landed gently on his head. At the same moment the phone rang. It was Lynne, so I handed him the receiver and he carried on the entire conversation upside down.

The magnifier from the CNIB has been a big success, relieving me from dictation sessions and allowing Dad to get back to his manuscript.

"Hey!", he says, "I've decided to go back to the original title."

"Oh, good!", I reply. "I've always preferred Land of Triangles as a title."

"No! Trainwatchers!" he shouts as he gropes down his trousers to scratch his belly.

I glance at the papers under the magnifier. All I see is a newsletter from the residents' council meeting.

The Resident Counsel (sic) Minutes

-Residents requested more raisins in their rice pudding. More have been added, however, still not enough.

-Residents inquired why the silverware is not very shiny.

-The sharp knives at mealtime are nice. Residents feel that the other knives are only good to butter buns.

-A resident mentioned that the food was hotter when the male cook worked here.

-Residents feel that the table decorations are too high. They find it difficult to see the person sitting across from them.

There is a knock at the door and in comes Sally, the manager, accompanied by two workmen. They have come to replace the bathroom floor. Dad is ogling Sally, who is very fit.

"I'm just admiring your figure." He doesn't care about his bathroom floor.

"For a legally blind man you sure see a lot!", she counters.

I decide to make my exit as the men begin to tear up the floor. Dad has enough distraction for the moment and I have just had enough.

Excerpt from Land of Triangles a.k.a Trainwatchers

Meanwhile for me sleep is out of the question. I head downstairs and find Amanda Todd in the kitchen. Now my head turns on again. It tells me how nice it would be to kiss her, to carry her off to bed...yes indeed, it would be far better in bed with Amanda---and I know this is a shocking time to think about it. We are not at that point yet and it will likely stay that way. Our relationship is purely professional and the closest we've come to intimacy is that we use first names now.

Chapter 24
Francy and the Glasses

I like to read the obits. They are rich with implied stories, a life remembered with dates and names. I just came across one that I thought might interest Dad. The man had been the husband of a woman who had worked with Dad at National Business. Her name is Francy. I read the obit to Dad.

"So, she's still alive then! How wonderful!"

The fact of her husband's passing was of no concern to Dad. They may never have met.

"I had always admired that woman. Not in a sexual way though. She was a very classy lady, excellent posture. At the office we had this little routine between us. She would come to my desk and borrow my glasses, then return them a little while later. Nothing was ever said…just a bit of a flirt, I suppose. Hey! Do you think you could find out where she is? I'd love to talk with her again. You know, about old times."

One of the problems about living so long is that there are very few people left to reminisce with in a meaningful way. Most of the "Natbus" crowd are gone. But there is one woman, Flora, who used to be his secretary and who still writes to Dad from time to time. I write his replies for him now. Maybe she can help find Francy. I hope so because now Dad is becoming obsessed with finding her.

I find Flora's number in Manitoba and get her on the line, explain why I'm calling and hand the phone to Dad. Flora suggests another woman to call, Marjorie, and gives me her number. Feeling foolish I call Marjorie. Bingo! She has it as well as Francy's address. I write it down in big print and hand it to Dad. He can do as he likes. I'm going home.

A few days later I get a call from Dad. He's all excited. He has talked with Francy. He asked her if she remembered the glasses. She did not. But they had a nice chat anyway. I hoped he didn't sound too gleeful at the fact that her husband had just died. The glasses in question are still in Dad's desk, along with several other pair. Maybe if she saw them she would remember?

My next task was to wrap the bloody glasses and send them to the poor woman, along with a note. I did. Dad continues to hope for a phone call but so far remains disappointed. And recently he told me he's not so sure it was Francy who borrowed the glasses after all. That might explain a lot.

Chapter 25
Magic

During the Fifties Dad made business trips to New York City. He took the opportunity to enjoy some Broadway Musicals and would return with the playbills and often the albums. Record albums back then were exactly that: a collection of 78's made of Bakelite discs, (breakable), arranged inside sleeves which formed a sort of book. Each disc was titled and numbered on a circular label in the center. I was allowed to stack the discs on our record player spindle and thus be able to listen to the entire score from South Pacific while recovering from the measles. The next year it was mumps and Guys and Dolls. I still remember most of the words and tunes. But don't ask me to sing.

One Christmas Eve Mom and Dad called Lynne and me downstairs to see something magical. It was completely dark. We could feel their presence in a corner of the kitchen but all we could see were three ghostly-greenish shapes. Bells, dancing bells, rising and falling by themselves. How enchanting! Even though we knew it was our parents doing the choreography we continued to act suitably impressed. Then Dad turned the lights back on and demonstrated how, by holding these plastic bells over a lightbulb they would magically absorb some of that light and could be seen again in the dark. Wow! What a great trick to show our friends. And it was.

And after the Christmas bells came the Christmas balls. These tree decorations were fashioned by winding strips of crepe paper around tiny toys such as paper parachutes, plastic cars, tin frogs that hopped, whistles and paper umbrellas. At the center was a Mexican jumping bean. On Christmas morning we unfurled the crepe paper streamers as out popped the little treasures. It took me a while to realise that the jumping bean was really a plastic capsule with a ball bearing inside. Lynne had taken hers apart to see the worm inside and the mystery was no more. Oh, well.

Then there was the egg trick. My boys loved that one. It wasn't so much magic but dramatic science. Grampa Jack would collect his props: a wooden stool, a glass milk bottle partly filled with water, a tin pie-plate, a small cardboard matchbox sheath, a straw broom and a raw egg. With great showmanship he would place the milk bottle on the stool, the pie tin over the bottle, the matchbox sheath standing vertically on the pie tin with the raw egg balanced on top. Then he would stand far back, grab the broom and lunge toward the setup, smacking the broom over the edge of the pie tin. Clang! The pie tin hit the ceiling. Plop! The egg landed inside the milk bottle, intact. It would make a great YouTube video today but try finding a glass milk bottle or a straw broom these days.

Here's another excerpt from Land of Triangles which has a magical quality.

In my mind's eye I can see it, those little tins careening right along, taking the fast water below Partridge Run, bumping into each other, tinkling and chattering like wind-chimes, elbowing and shoving each other, thousands of them, until a natural sense of order shapes their passage. Little by little rust and the river will get them.

This lyrical passage describes the deliberate destruction of a fortunes' worth of cocaine which is what those tinkling tins contained. This is near the end of his novel and everything is working out as it should. Like magic.

Chapter 26
Lies and a Lesson for Life

My father has been busy lately. He claims to have finished reading Land of Triangles and deems it fit to send out to a publisher.

"You know, it's a damn good book", he declares, "no need to make any changes. I've so enjoyed reading it again. I had completely forgotten what it was about. It's even better than I thought. Let's send it out and see what happens!"

And so, the lies begin. I am amazed at how well I do it. Several days later I tell him that I have sent a query letter to a publisher in Ottawa. That should buy me some time while I work on this, my book about *his* book. But it has become more than that, of course. It's a book about him. When he does eventually find out---and I do intend to tell him---I think he will be pleased. There is nobody more interesting to my father than my father.

One winter evening, when I was about eleven, I had come home from the skating rink in tears during an adolescent meltdown because "nobody wants to skate with me, nobody likes me!" But instead of a reassuring hug and a 'there, there, dear', what I got was a pep-talk from Dad, one I have never forgotten.

"You have to make the effort to talk to the others. Don't always expect them to come up to you… ask them how they are, engage them in conversation. If you show that you're interested in them they will want to be with you. Remember, there is nothing more important to a person than him or herself. Learn to be a good listener...people love to talk about themselves. Now, get those skates back on and go over to the skating rink. See if I'm right!"

I did and he was. I ended up having a wonderful time with another girl whom I didn't know well and found her to be fun and interesting. I came home elated. Years later, Dad confessed to me how he had secretly followed me to the rink and watched from behind a snowbank, afraid that maybe he had been too harsh but relieved to see that the lesson had been a good one.

I recently reminded him of that episode and suggested that perhaps he should take his own advice. He had been complaining about the lack of interesting conversation with other residents at The Lodge. "They're either mutes or bingo-heads. They have nothing to say. I prefer my own company."

I'm afraid it's true. Jonathan/Jamieson/Jack really is a loner. And a romantic. He was always trying to find ways to impress Phyllis, not an easy thing to do. He used to joke that he could bring home the moon and she would say," Just put it in the corner. I'm making dinner." But it was always Phyllis who forged the social ties, a not uncommon reality in most relationships. I wish my father were a bit more outgoing and friendly with the other residents instead of trying to mow them down with his wheelchair if they get in his way down the corridor or cursing them during bingo games or religious services. But he won't change. People don't, really. As we age, we just become more of what we always were.

Chapter 27
Noodling

"Hey, Dad, want to go for a noodle? In my new car?"

He doesn't think twice. Spins around in his wheelchair and heads for the corridor. I push him along. He likes it even though he can propel himself very well using his feet. I punch in the code at the main doors and we're out on the patio.

"Wait there. I'll go get the car."

"Do you think I'm going anywhere else?"

I drive up to the patio in my brand-new candy-apple red car. Dad is seeing it for the first time though he knew about it. It was at his insistence and with his generosity that I was able to buy it. I help him slide into the seat, buckle him up and off we go.

"Ahh...that wonderful new- car smell!"

We head north along Highway 34 towards Hawkesbury.

"And it holds the road like it's attached by a magnet. I love the colour. Nice choice, Kid!"

We pull in at the Dairy Queen. I have prepared for this: towels, wipes and garbage bags because we'll be having our treats inside the car and I want to avoid spills on the new interior. I go inside and order. Dad wants a cherry sundae with chocolate sauce, I get myself a shake. He dives right into the sundae with his usual gusto...I'm glad I have the wipes. We talk and slurp.

"Dad, I want you to know how much Lynne and I appreciate your generosity. You've always had deep pockets."

"Hell, it's never been a fortune. But I've always believed money is there to be spent and enjoyed as long as there's enough for the basics. And now that I've reached this ridiculously old age---I'm what they call an over-stayer---I can't use the money on myself anymore but I can enjoy giving it to you and Lynne."

"Yeah, we're getting our inheritance while you're still here. Your job now is to stay alive as long as possible and enjoy our enjoyment. But really... you've always been generous. There was always some pretty good swag under the Christmas tree. Lynne and I believed in Santa for a long time because we thought you could never afford to give us so much. Later Mom told me about the Christmas Club which she paid into every month. So, it was both of you. "

We're down to the last licks now. No disasters on the car seats that I can see. We continue on our noodle. As a teenager I loved going for a Saturday morning noodle with Dad. There was a new shopping center in Dorval, what would today be considered a large strip-mall, but back then it was special. I could prowl around the shops, maybe purchase a record or two, then meet Dad by the hot-dog stand near Pascal's. We had a little dog, Mam'selle, who happily rode with us in anticipation of a new red, white and blue rubber ball. That dog went through one ball a week, chewing it to shreds. You could pick up a tiny shred, pitch it out into the field of long grass and she would find it.

I take the long road back, the shun-pike roads that Dad loves. At every turn he has a tale to tell. I can anticipate them all. We drive slowly past The Farmette, their last house before moving to The Hermitage. Now we're curving around Cassburn Road and head east along through Vankleek Hill on the Barb Road. Dad realises we've passed The Hermitage and are now driving towards The Farm. "Wouldn't it be fun to see the old house?", he suggests hopefully. He doesn't know that I've already made arrangements to visit with the present owners. We turn up the long driveway and park by the old shed where Dad kept his tractor. The owner comes out to welcome us and invites us inside but I decline her kind offer. Dad is not steady on his feet and is happy just to look around outside. So much growth since they left eleven years ago. Dad spies the old Papoe cedar leaning valiantly by the hydro pole. That tree has had a long and interesting life. It was first planted as a young spindly shrub by my grandfather when we lived in Baie d"Urfe. It survived being uprooted and replanted in Toronto, then in Hudson and finally at The Farm. It was too big to move to Greenlane so it stays at The Farm, where it looks as if it will soon die. The weeping willow, however, is thriving down by the creek. It's enormous.

We thank the owner and drive slowly away. It's close to dinner time for Dad.

"I would have liked to go inside," says Dad, "but

maybe it's just as well we didn't. I know it would look different, not how I remember it."

"My thoughts as well. Best to leave it alone. We did see the Papoe cedar...that was enough, don't you think?"

Chapter 28
A Discovery

A week later I'm back at The Lodge with more supplies: AA batteries, hearing-aid batteries, a recent photo of his great-grandchildren, some chocolate covered cherries and a box of Poly Grip. As I clean the hearing aids, I learn that his lower plate is missing.

"It's somewhere around, probably under the desk.", he guesses. I start poking around, check on the floor, the drawers, under his pillow. It's quite possible his lower plate has been nudged off his desk and fallen into his waste basket, never to be seen again.

"Never mind, it'll turn up. I only use it when we have corn on the cob and that's not very often. Oh, but guess what! I found another manuscript!"

"Really? Which one?"

"It's called Body Movements. It was in a box under the desk. I'd completely forgotten about it. I've been reading it and I think it's even better than Trainwatchers. So we have a lot of work ahead of us."

Oh no! He's talking about *that* one. I haven't read much of it, too put off by frequent references to the *oberfeldwebel und Operation Wandervogel*. But I feign interest. He continues, fired up by this new discovery. "There's this cat called Paula, except nobody knows she's a cat till the end and then she gets impaled by a shard of broken glass during the explosion. That's how it ends. Except I don't know what to do about Robert. He ends up with two women. That won't do. I'll have to fix that."

I make a suggestion. "Why don't you kill Robert instead of the cat?"

"Yes! Good idea! That might work. I'm going to dictate a new ending."

"Deal!"

Chapter 29
Walter

Dad liked to name certain inanimate objects. His typewriter was Betsy-Ann, his mandolin, hauled out at party time, was Mabel. Then there was Walter.

By definition, a Walter is any objet d'art of dubious aesthetic quality. Kitsch would be another descriptor.

It was on my ninth Christmas that I saw my first Walter. Under the pine boughs of our tree lay this strangely wrapped gift. It was lumpy and rattled when we poked it. "From Our House to Your House" read the tag, from a distant relative. Dad asked Mom to do the honours. She unwrapped it slowly. Being a paper-saver, this was her way. Agonising. At last, the thing was exposed. She held it up for us to wonder and admire...what *was* it?

Imagine a cluster of hollow gourds and seedpods, painted in bright tropical hues, dusted with glitter, entwined with raffia, all cascading from a huge velvet bow from which to hang it from any handy hook. We had no words.

Then Dad, recognising the potential for mirth, moved we adopt it. He christened it "Walter" and hung it over our dining room table from the brass rosette where once had hung a chandelier. We ate our Christmas dinner under Walter. When guests would arrive during the holiday they would chortle in amusement, often making some humourous comment.

Walter was put away after Christmas but whenever an impromptu party erupted---a fairly common occurrence---suddenly Walter appeared.

When we moved from that house of my childhood Walter was left behind. Perhaps he had rotted away or had lost too many seed-pods. But his legend survived.

Chapter 30
My Father's Bastards

Dad needs new pajamas. Mom used to buy them at a local men's wear shop that has closed. They are polo pajamas and, as he says, "I wear the bastards all day now. They are comfortable and don't really look like pajamas. Can you get me some new ones? These ones are getting quite shabby."

Indeed, they were. So off I went to find polo pajamas. No luck in any of our stores here, including Walmart. I called my sister. "Do you think you can find polo pajamas anywhere near you? You know, the ones he calls his bastards?"

A week later a parcel arrived. With a note. *Two pairs of Dad's bastards.*

Oh joy! I delivered them right away, a grey pair and a blue pair, along with a box of chocolate-covered cherries. Dad was ecstatic. Such simple things now to please my father.

Chapter 31
Almost New Year's Eve

My cousin, Sue, and her teenage daughter, Michelle, were visiting from Vancouver between Christmas and New Year. Sue's mother and mine were sisters. Both had passed on but our fathers were still with us. Sue and Michie had made a special trip to Vankleek Hill to visit us. When they arrived in their rented car Sue asked, "Should we go now to see Uncle Jack or do you want to wait till tomorrow?"

"Now, I think." I replied. It was a good decision. It was early evening as we drove over to The Lodge. We entered Dad's room to find him almost prone in his lounge chair, half asleep. He rallied when he saw us and tried to become more animated but I could see it was an effort. He was short of breath and struggled to engage in conversation so after a short exchange of family news and holiday cheer I signalled to Sue that we should leave. Dad wanted to see us off so I wheeled him down the corridor to the lounge. The Christmas tree was still up and lit. Beneath it was the little electric train set Dad had purchased years ago and donated to The Lodge. Dad smiled at the scene. He was still wearing his blue "bastards". We hugged, waved goodbye and left.

It was still dark, early the next morning, when the phone rang. It was the nurse from The Lodge who, in a calm but firm voice, began, "Your father... he's not been doing so well."

"I know, he's been down with pneumonia again."

"Yes, well, … he came down from his room earlier this morning asking for a glass of milk. He wheeled himself back and a bit later I went to check on him. He had died. The police are here and want to talk with you."

Wow! I had expected to hear that Dad was in hospital. I lay in shock while the police officer asked me if I wanted to see his body before they took him away.

"No, I saw him last night. That's the memory I want to keep."

I got up and went to the kitchen. I needed coffee and I needed to be alone. By now George was up and asked, wordlessly, about the phone call. Wordlessly I answered. George understood and went back to bed. I sat in the living room and gathered my thoughts and emotions. My father, aged ninety-seven, is dead. I was grateful for having seen him last evening, smiling at the little train under the tree, wearing his blue bastards, grateful that he had died in his own bed, sad that he was gone.

It was still early morning when I called my sister. All I could say was "Dad."

Chapter 32
Celebration of Life

On July 22, his birthday, we drove Dad's ashes to the Barb Road Cemetery. My little red car led the cortege. My son, Andrew, drove, with his fiancée, Jordan, and son, Finn in the front. I sat in the back with my granddaughter, Alberta. Dad's urn sat between us. They represented the Calgary contingent. Following us were Lynne, Frank and Joanna from Warkworth and Melissa and Mike from Toronto. My son Jon, from Montreal, rode with them. Then came Sue and Michie from Vancouver and Uncle Don from Pincourt, Quebec. Cousins Steve and Cindy from Kitchener gave George a lift and Dad's sister, Irene, with daughter Jacqui, from Toronto, were next. My friend and former neighbour, Monique, completed the parade.

We parked in the field outside the cemetery which is surrounded by pines, a welcome source of shade on that hot day of high summer. We gathered by the gravesite and were met by Harvey and Sheila Leroy, former neighbours of my parents. They brought flowers and had arranged for the ground to be opened by the gravestone, the one with the ivy garland surrounding the locomotive engine.

I began by addressing the wooden urn---such a surreal feeling to think of my father in there---I related a few stories and invited others to speak. Andrew stepped up and related the tale of the Oshawa Rock. I was choked up and proud that he had remembered his Grampa telling him that long-ago experience of being a young man who suddenly realises that he is responsible for his own survival. It was a fitting anecdote.

Then we lowered the urn and everyone took turns covering the grave with earth, tucking him in.

Back at our house we celebrated Dad's life. We played his favourite music, much Gershwin, of course. We ate food from his favourite restaurant, Stephanie's, we listened while the musicians in the family, Melissa and Mike on sax and Jon on guitar, played a small concert in tribute, we raised many toasts and I was finally able to relax and enjoy the support of family and friends. It was a huge comfort to know we had done right by Dad. I felt his spirit there that day and I know he approved.

Chapter 33
Dear Dad

Dear Dad,

Well now…this has taken a lot longer than I had thought but now I think this weaving project is complete. I hope you like the finished textile; your words and mine, the warp and the weft, fashioned as whole fabric. Colourful, I think. And textured. It's been ten years since you moved on into the ethers, but I still feel you watching.

I hope you are still enjoying your time in that special garage you once told me about, the one in your dream with a secret warehouse that stored a huge locomotive engine. I bet you take your special people there to show it to them. There will be many of these, mainly women: Your mother, Jessie, my mother, Phyllis, your young loves, Bella and Helga, some older ones too who shall remain nameless. I also hope you finally found your own father, Valentine Smith, who died before ever meeting you. You often wondered what kind of person he had been; your mother never gave you much to go on.

But I have been luckier. You shared so much with Lynne and me; your experiences, your dreams, your weaknesses (yes, sometimes you were a bit of a horse's ass), and your successes. You gave the best advice. I didn't always take it, but upon reflection later, I knew it was good. You saw me through two marriages, two careers and you engaged well with my two sons, Jon and Andrew.

I remember one conversation we had while I was going through an emotionally troubled time. You suggested that I should be with a poet. Well, now I am. But you know this, of course, as you float around in your lava lamp. And you probably also know that this poet is a retired plumber. This will no doubt appeal to your practical nature.

It was at the suggestion or rather the strong urging of this plumber-poet that I finally put these words together as a gift to you and to myself.

Thank you, Dad. And thank you, Jerry.

Love,

Fran

Jack, 1920. (Toronto)

Jack and his mother, Jessie.

Phyllis, 1940.

Jack, Fran and Gramma Deragon, 1943.
(Ste-Anne-de-Bellevue)

Jack, broadcasting on BBC, 1944.

Jack and Phyllis, 1949.

Fran, Jack (wearing his 'Bastards'), 2013.

www.ingramcontent.com/pod-product-compliance
Lightning Source LLC
Chambersburg PA
CBHW070547090426
42735CB00013B/3101